# BEST PRACTICES ARE STUPID

---

## 40 WAYS TO OUT-INNOVATE THE COMPETITION

### STEPHEN M. SHAPIRO

an imprint of Amplify | Publishing Group

www.amplifypublishing.com

*Best Practices Are Stupid: 40 Ways to Out-Innovate the Competition*

*www.StephenShapiro.com*

*To all the individuals and companies I've worked with over the years. Your stories, struggles, and insights have been my greatest teachers.*

# CONTENTS

# PREFACE TO UPDATED EDITION
## WHAT I DIDN'T HAVE TIME TO INCLUDE IN THE ORIGINAL BOOK

On May 4, 2011, we were only days away from going to press with my fifth book, yet it still did not have a title. I provided nearly one hundred different ideas, and the publisher rejected them all. They had a title they wanted to use, but I didn't like it. I was told they would run with theirs if I could not find a title they liked better. The clock was ticking.

At the eleventh hour, on a phone call with them, I suggested the title, *Best Practices Are Stupid.* The line went quiet. And then I heard, "Ok, we'll go with that."

There's a problem with choosing a title at the last minute. The title should have a solid link to the book's theme. Although tip 18 is "Best Practices Are (Sometimes) Stupid," that was only one small slice of the book, and it focused more on when to use best practices – not why they are a bad idea.

Given the last-minute change, I could only make minor edits to the introduction to reflect the new title.

Therefore, I added this brief preface for this edition, sharing the three reasons best practices are stupid. Although some of this is referenced in the introduction, I felt it would be good to include all of it here in one place.

## #1: Innovation is Not Replication

If you are trying to differentiate your organization and using a best practice, you'll be playing a game of catch-up.

By the time you implement someone else's best practice, they're on to the next one. You can't differentiate your organization by replicating what someone else is doing.

Unless you strive to compete primarily on price, being a copycat is rarely a solid strategy.

## #2: Context Matters

We often believe we can take a practice from one organization and bring it to another. But culture, resources, competitive position, industry, and other contextual factors matter.

It seems as though everyone wants to be like Amazon or Apple. But let's face it; you most likely don't have their reach, scale, or financial position. Therefore, replicating a practice from an organization like that makes no sense for most companies.

Is your organization hierarchical or flat? Does your culture encourage risk-taking, or is it risk-averse? Are you centralized or decentralized? All of these determine if practices may apply to your organization.

Your business differentiator impacts which practices make sense for your organization. Your geography, business strategy, management approach, organization structure, industry, and more will affect which practices might be useful.

The bottom line: context and culture matter.

## #3: Lack of Causation

While speaking at a conference several years ago, I tried an experiment. I told the audience that I had discovered the five best practices that nearly all successful people have in common. I printed these practices on a sheet of paper and invited ten successful people from the audience to join me on stage.

I asked each of these individuals how many of these practices they used in their personal life or business. It turns out that all five practices were used by all ten of these successful entrepreneurs.

The audience gasped. They were on the edge of their seats, waiting to hear the keys to the kingdom. I then read off the five practices:

- Read your email (at least) once a day
- Smile (at least) once a day
- Brush your teeth (nearly) every day
- Shower (at least) twice a week
- Wear clothes to work

Although the successful entrepreneurs all laughed, the audience was disappointed.

But it made an important point. Any time you hear about a best practice, make sure you consider if it was the true cause of success rather than a coincidence or correlation.

## The Undersampling of Failure

For my experiment, I found ten successful people knowing they would have used these silly practices. But had I taken the time to look, I would certainly have found people in the audience who used those exact practices yet weren't nearly as successful.

This is called the "undersampling of failure" (a.k.a. Survivorship Bias). We tend to focus on the winners and successes, but we don't take time to track down the times when advice or a best practice didn't work.

Companies that were successful in implementing a particular practice are at conferences talking about their experiences. They write books about their approaches. But what about the hundreds or thousands of companies that did exactly the same practice and failed? We don't hear about them. They're not being invited to speak at conferences or to write books.

We focus on those who did well, but we don't spend time investigating the people who tried that same practice and weren't successful. Why can a practice have both successes and failures? To answer this, we need to distinguish causation from correlation and coincidence.

### Causation, Correlation, and Coincidence

Causation means that the given practice was the actual cause of a company's success. If they didn't apply this practice, they would not have achieved the results they did.

But in many cases, the relationship between a practice and success is not causation but rather correlation or coincidence.

Coincidence means there is no relationship. The silly practices I shared had little or no relationship to someone's success. Of course, if you never brush your teeth, never smile, and never read your email, it might prevent you from being successful. But doing these things will certainly not create success.

Correlation is best explained with a simple example.

Let's assume that the following statement is true: "Individuals with greater wealth are happier."

Most people reading this will jump to the conclusion that money makes people happy. In doing so, they assume that money is the cause of happiness. If we make money, we become happy.

But research shows that this is not the case. Money does not cause happiness; happiness creates wealth. The happier someone is, the more they are eager to work and the more people want to work with them.

Wealth and happiness are correlated. But money doesn't cause happiness; happiness causes wealth. The wrong causation leads people to chase wealth in the belief that they'll be happy, and they're never happy.

Understanding the distinction between causation, correlation, and coincidence is critical for innovation. If you're going to apply a supposed best practice, you had better understand that the work that you're doing and the money you're investing will cause the success you want.

Sometimes, even when there is a causation, other considerations may influence their usefulness. For example, timing can also be a factor. In today's fast-moving world, studying what someone did last year may be irrelevant to what will work today. People teaching you social media strategies may be outdated by the time you hear about them. I've had my own business for over twenty years. The approaches that I used in the past to drive my success would be silly in today's environment.

And in some cases, a first-mover advantage may be the cause. The first people on social media had a better chance of making it big than those joining today. And those who hopped on the Bitcoin bandwagon early on will certainly make more money than those who decide to invest there now.

These concepts are critical for all organizations (and individuals) to understand. We love to learn from others. And we should because it can speed development times. But remember, replication is never innovation. Replicating someone else's practices without skepticism can lead to failure.

---

*Best Practices Are Stupid* was originally published by Penguin Portfolio in 2011. 800-CEO-READ (now Porchlight), the premier distributor of business books, chose it as the best innovation and creativity book of that year. It was even the number one best-selling business book in Canada, according to The Globe and Mail.

However, ten years have passed since then.

In 2020, I published my sixth book, *Invisible Solutions: 25 Lenses that Reframe and Help Solve Difficult Business Problems* (Amplify Publishing, 2020). At that time, my efforts shifted to the newer book, and I stopped promoting this one.

I had moved on. Or so I thought.

Although I wasn't actively publicizing *Best Practices Are Stupid*, I found myself referring back to this book frequently when involved in deeper transformational work with my clients. The newer book extensively discusses one step of the innovation process: reframing. Although this is a critical step that companies often get wrong, *Invisible Solutions* doesn't address all the topics needed for the broader cultural shift. But *Best Practices Are Stupid* does. It covers nearly every aspect of innovation, including organization models, metrics, investment strategies, open innovation, motivation strategies, and more.

Admittedly, some examples may seem outdated a decade after its publication. However, the concepts behind each story remain valid a decade later. Therefore, for this revised edition, I decided to keep the essence of the original book, only making minor edits. And instead of changing the core text, I added "author's notes" at the end of each chapter. These provide additional thoughts not included in the original book.

In addition, I added a new chapter at the end that details the process we used to create a 20,000-person process and innovation practice at the consulting firm Accenture. We did this in only nine months. You might find this model helpful for delivering massive and rapid change within your organization.

I hope you enjoy reading this. Happy innovating.

Stephen Shapiro
inquries@stephenshapiro.com
www.stephenshapiro.com

# INTRODUCTION

On April 20, 2010, the environment was dealt a horrific blow. On that day, the Deepwater Horizon oil rig exploded, spewing as much as 180 million gallons of crude oil into the Gulf Coast of the United States. It took eighty-seven days to cap the gushing wellhead.

In the weeks following the explosion, scientists, movie stars, and concerned citizens tried to devise ways to slow the flow. But workable solutions were hard to find and implement, as the well was nearly a mile below the ocean's surface. Repeated attempts failed.

In an effort to find better solutions, the Deepwater Horizon Unified Command, spearheaded by BP, launched a website where anyone could submit their ideas in an online suggestion box. According to USA Today, the website received nearly 125,000 ideas; 80,000 suggestions were for plugging the leak, and 43,000 were for ways to clean up the oil.

Of these ideas, one hundred were deemed as having some merit, and a couple of dozen were tested.

On the surface, this might appear to have been a successful

endeavor; BP was able to gather lots of possible ideas to help end the disaster.

For a company that stood to lose billions of dollars in cleanup costs, relief payouts, and lost sales due to bad publicity, this approach might indeed have been a good strategy.

But the resources necessary to respond to this type of disaster typically don't exist within most organizations. Although a workable solution may have been found using this strategy, it is unclear if that was the case. Regardless, consider how many people it would take to evaluate thousands of ideas. If one person could evaluate an idea in thirty seconds (which is optimistic, especially for a technically complex issue like this) and could dedicate forty hours a week to the task, it would take over half a year to evaluate that many submissions. This would be a significant investment for any company.

With an innovation strategy like this, finding a useful idea is like finding a needle in a haystack. Or, more accurately, it is like finding a specific needle in a stack of other needles.

Unfortunately, this innovation strategy is what many well-intentioned companies use in their quest to be more innovative. They operate under the misguided belief that getting more ideas leads to better innovation. Organizations that use this approach spend too much time sorting the wheat from the chaff. And sadly, most of the ideas are chaff.

As this book will reveal, you don't want more ideas. You want to focus on finding solutions to pressing problems that enable your company to be more innovative. In fact, I'll teach you why the key to innovating *successfully* involves innovating *efficiently*.

The popular press and innovation gurus often provide well-worn examples that muddy the waters on how to approach the innovation process.

Google reportedly lets its employees use 20 percent of their time to develop new ideas. "PhDs and other smarty pants agreed to hand over their brains to the search giant for four days of the week and, in return, they were given the fifth to work on any project of their fancy." Many experts hold this up as an effective way to innovate. In actuality, this investment was designed to help Google win the "war for talent" and did little to generate new revenue streams. Despite the enormous investment, 97 percent of their revenues still come from advertising, the same way they have always made money.

3M uses a similar strategy, giving employees 15 percent of their time to explore. When discussing the 15 percent rule, someone from 3M once told me, "Which fifteen percent? I work sixty hours a week and there's no time for my fifteen percent." The answer appears to involve working weekends, as Les Krogh, retired senior vice president of Research and Development once said, "If 3Mers have to get something done, they'll do it. They'll take their 15 percent on Saturdays or Sundays, if need be."

Admittedly, their approach has indeed produced some fantastic innovations. But will this strategy work for your organization? Both Google and 3M benefit from a highly motivated workforce that is probably more ambitious than employees in most organizations.

Is there a more efficient way for you to innovate?

Allowing employees to dedicate 15 percent to 20 percent of their time to the innovation efforts of their choosing is akin to the infinite monkey theorem: if you give an infinite amount of monkeys an infinite number of typewriters, they would eventually write *War and Peace*. The belief is that if you give employees enough time to tinker around and develop enough harebrained ideas, they will eventually find the next big innovation (and no, I am not suggesting that your employees are monkeys).

Although this might yield new ideas, it is hardly an efficient way to innovate.

Let's face it, the old innovation models are broken, inefficient, and fail to produce results. It's time for you to innovate the way you innovate and apply some new thinking to your innovation process.

This book comprises forty tips designed to help you do just

that. These tips are designed to help you innovate differently. Innovate more efficiently. Innovate in a more focused manner.

Some tips are intended to change the way you think about innovation. Others are designed to change how you innovate. Depending on your experience level, you may already be familiar with some tips, while others will be new concepts for even the most advanced innovation practitioners. Some tips are primarily useful at an organizational level, while others are essential for all individuals to consider.

In some cases, you may not agree with my point of view. That's ok! The objective of each tip is to get you and your team thinking. You don't necessarily need to take what I say at face value. Challenge each concept. Discuss them. See how they apply to your organization. There is no one-size-fits-all solution for innovation. Pick and choose the tips that will have the most significant impact.

Although the tips are organized in a logical sequence, they can be read in any order, and each stands on its own. The first series of tips introduce some of the most important concepts relating to "innovating the way you innovate," and the remainder of the book is loosely organized around the components of the innovation capability: process, strategy, measures, people, and technology:

- *Process*: Most innovation efforts are ineffective and unfocused. To remedy this, you will be introduced to challenge-centered innovation, an efficient process for solving your most pressing issues and opportunities.
- *Strategy*: If you don't understand your customer's latent desires, your innovation effort will be comparable to a wild goose chase. Armed with their actual wants and needs, you can develop a powerful innovation strategy.
- *Measures*: Your measurement systems may inadvertently be killing your innovation efforts. You can stimulate creativity and foster innovation by making simple changes to your motivation strategy.

- *People*: Innovation depends on having the right people – with divergent points of view - in the right roles. The key is to treat each individual like an owner of the business, pushing decision-making to the lowest levels of the organization.
- *Creativity*: One aspect of the people dimension is competency. With innovation, one specific competency involves the ability to develop creative solutions. Although creativity is technically part of the "people" dimension of the innovation capability, given its importance, I have dedicated a section to these techniques. These can be used in brainstorming sessions or as instructional aids for helping people be more creative.
- *Technology*: Technology is critical in finding solutions to challenges and enabling collaboration. Although this is a distinct component of the innovation capability, the world of technology is changing so rapidly. Therefore, anything written in a book would be immediately obsolete. Given this, I chose not to focus on it in this book.

I am always amazed by the high quality of people employed by companies around the world. I am even more amazed by how little most companies tap into the innovative potential of these employees. This book provides dozens of proven tips and techniques that will enable you to get the most out of your workforce.

Innovation is the key to long-term growth. Although many companies are enamored with utilizing best practices, as this book's title suggests, duplicating what others are already doing relegates you to a continuous game of catch-up. Following in the footsteps of others is the fastest way to irrelevancy. Instead, create your own path. Find new and creative ways of staying ahead of the competition. An organization can only survive and thrive in today's volatile marketplace through repeated, rapid, and efficient change.

 **With most innovation strategies, finding a good idea is like finding a specific needle in a stack of other needles.**

*AUTHOR'S NOTE: 3M is an excellent example of why context matters regarding best practices. Their 15 percent rule works for them because they have decades of experience. It's a powerful strategy for their organization as it is part of their DNA. And their employees are eager to find the next big product innovation. Unfortunately, other companies that try to replicate this approach often waste 15 percent of their time and money on innovations that add no value. 3M's culture and measurement systems are designed to support this concept; yours is probably not.*

# OVERVIEW

## INNOVATE THE WAY YOU INNOVATE

Before diving into the specifics of the innovation capability, let's review some key innovation concepts. Not everyone will share my point of view in this section. That's expected as these tips challenge the "conventional wisdom" that dominates popular thought. However, the high failure rate of most innovation efforts tells us that these conventional approaches may not be so wise after all. Ready? Let's get started.

# 1

## NOT SURVIVAL OF THE FITTEST – SURVIVAL OF THE ADAPTABLE

Have you heard the one about two men who are hiking through the mountains of Canada? The story goes that after stumbling upon a hungry, 600-pound grizzly bear, one of the hikers removes his backpack and hiking boots and puts on his running shoes. The other hiker looks at him and asks, "What are you doing? You can't outrun a bear!" The first hiker responds, "I know, but I only need to outrun you!"

This story highlights the essence of innovation. Innovation is not about new products, new processes, new services, new business models, or even new ideas. It is about staying one step ahead of your competition so you are not eaten. Let's face it; there are a lot of hungry competitors out there. And when you are trying to outpace the bear (your current competition), you must ensure you don't run into an alligator or a tiger (your new competition).

Innovation is about change. Not a one-time change but ongoing change. It is about adaptability, flexibility, and agility.

Consider this...

When the pace of change outside your organization is greater than the pace of change within, you will be eaten and have difficulty keeping your business afloat. And as you know, the rate of change outside your organization is faster than ever.

The *only* way to survive is to stop treating innovation as a one-time event. Innovation must be a continuous, never-ending process. The second you rest on your laurels, you can be sure someone will catch you for breakfast.

But the story of the two hikers does not end with the first hiker saying, "I only need to outrun you." It continues with the second hiker saying, "Go ahead and try," and then he stands perfectly still as the first hiker takes off. The second hiker smiles because he knows bears have poor eyesight and will only chase prey that runs away. The first hiker gets eaten. The second hiker reflects on the importance of understanding the hunting habits of large carnivores–and of choosing friends wisely.

The moral of the story is that, although organizations want to speed up their innovation efforts and move quickly, running in the wrong direction can actually slow you down and burn valuable resources. Instead, take deliberate action. Know what will improve your business. Understand the marketplace and harness the energies of your organization by focusing on what is most important.

And yes, pick your friends–and colleagues–wisely. Choosing the right innovation partners is an important part of your innovation strategy.

So, what can an organization do to avoid getting eaten by the competition?

### The Three Levels of Innovation

The answer to that lies in a basic understanding of the three levels of innovation.

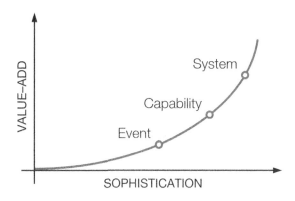

**LEVEL 1: INNOVATION AS AN EVENT:** This is where most companies find themselves. They conduct brainstorming sessions or hold random contests to generate new ideas. If a good idea is produced, some value is added to the organization. In some cases, the idea may even lead to tremendous value. However, a considerable amount of work generally needs to happen between idea generation and its realization.

**LEVEL 2: INNOVATION AS A CAPABILITY:** This is the next level of sophistication. The organization puts in place structures and processes to define problems, generate and evaluate solutions, and develop action plans to implement those solutions. The result is a realistic deliverable based on an organizational challenge or opportunity.

**LEVEL 3: INNOVATION AS A SYSTEM:** The ultimate level involves creating an environment where innovation is embedded in everything you do. At both the event- and capability-driven levels, innovation tends to be reactionary and discrete. It is somewhat separate from the business. With embedded innovation, people not only innovate to deal with "problems or challenges" that are presented to them but with everything they do. They continuously, even radically, improve their products, processes, and organization. This creates exponential and ongoing value.

## Where do you begin?

The first step is to create an environment where creativity is encouraged, and solutions are implemented in response to specific challenges. This is Level 2: innovation as a repeatable process and capability. In fact, a large portion of this book is dedicated to helping organizations achieve that level. Once this is mastered, you can more easily move on to innovation as a system: the Holy Grail of innovation.

Too often, organizations send employees to creativity classes. When these individuals return, they are excited about generating new ideas. Unfortunately, they are confronted with an environment that stifles creativity and innovation. They are told to keep their heads down and their mouths shut. There is no vehicle for tapping into their new creative energies. They become disgruntled and frustrated. Now you have a bigger morale problem. Creative ideas without an encouraging innovation environment lead to employee dissatisfaction. An overall shift towards a culture of innovation must be put in place before people can be trained to be creative thinkers.

Although people believe that Darwin suggested that it is the survival of the fittest, his perspective on "natural selection" was that it is not physical shape but rather the ability to adapt that is critical.

This is the goal of innovation. The smartest organization will not survive. The company with the most money can quickly fall from grace. But the organization that adapts and evolves to address ever-changing market conditions will thrive in the long run.

**When the pace of change outside your organization is greater than the pace of change within, you will be eaten.**

---

*AUTHOR'S NOTE: I have seen many organizations progress from Level 1 to Level 2 over the past decade. But as you will see in my Author's Note for the next tip, this doesn't mean it has positively impacted overall innovation. Having an innovation team does not mean your organization is innovative. In addition, there is a big difference between adaptability and non-stop change. Employees and leaders are suffering from innovation fatigue because companies value the pace of change over the clarity of direction. Purposeful change is more important than the speed or quantity of change initiatives. Moving quickly in the wrong direction only hurts the organization. In an attempt to outmaneuver the bear, companies have been spinning out of control.*

## 2

## HOW CAN YOU AVOID BECOMING A ONE-HIT WONDER?

D o you know the bands Lipps Inc, The Sugar Hill Gang, or Haddaway? You might know the song that each artist made famous: Funky Town, Rapper's Delight, and What is Love, respectively. These artists were "one-hit wonders." They climbed to the top of the music charts once and were never heard from again.

This is not too dissimilar to what happens with many businesses. They generate one good idea to gain momentum but quickly fall from grace. What can you do to prevent your organization from becoming a one-hit wonder? Make sure your innovation efforts are predictable and sustainable by treating them like any other capability in your company.

As an example, think about your organization's finance capability. It has skilled experts (e.g., CPAs), measures (e.g., Days Sales Outstanding), supporting technology (e.g., Oracle or SAP), processes (e.g., processes for closing the books at year-end), an owner (the CFO), and a strategy. Your innovation capability requires all of these elements, and more, including skilled innovation experts, innovation measures, innovation management technologies, an innovation process, an innovation "owner," and a clearly articulated innovation strategy.

With these pieces in place, you can begin to make innovation a repeatable and predictable process where creativity is encouraged throughout the organization and the best solutions are implemented. This is the second level of innovation described in the previous tip: "Innovation as a capability."

Five key components are required for successful long-term innovation:

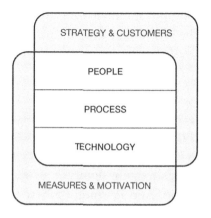

STRATEGY: A strategy is needed to decide when, where, and how innovation will be used within the organization. Most importantly, it should address "why" you want innovation. Are you looking primarily for a new pipeline of products? Do you want to serve your customers better? Are you looking to create a more nimble, flexible, and adaptable organization? For one company, the mantra for innovation was "2 x 10" - to become a two-billion-dollar business by 2010. This made it clear to all employees why innovation is needed and what it means to deliver innovative ideas. Another company solely focuses on its customers with the mantra, "Innovation is anything that makes the lives of our customers better."

. . .

**MEASURES:** Innovation, as with any capability, needs to be measurable and measured. You will want to measure the value of your innovation pipeline. Who will be measured? What kinds of measures will be used? How will you measure less tangible values such as adaptability? How will you relate innovation to overall business outcomes and results?

**PROCESS:** Innovation requires an end-to-end model for targeting, generating, selecting, and implementing innovative solutions. As you will discover, the recommended innovation process starts with a challenge and ends with value created for the organization.

**PEOPLE:** Your people are your culture. If you want a culture of innovation, your employees must embrace actions, values, beliefs, skills, and language consistent with this objective. Everyone, at all levels, must appreciate divergent points of view. Creativity must be encouraged and valued. And it would be best to have the proper organization and leadership models in place.

**TECHNOLOGY:** Innovative companies use collaboration tools to enable communication between employees, customers, suppliers, and external experts. Solutions are captured in ways that facilitate the dissemination and replication of innovative thinking. These technologies enable communication across all levels, organizations, and business boundaries.

You will notice that this book is organized chiefly around each of these components, providing even greater detail on how to implement an innovation capability in your organization.

For too long, innovation has been relegated to the darkest

recesses of Research and Development (R&D) departments and the conference rooms of well-meaning brainstormers. But now is the time to bring innovation to the forefront of your business. Now is the time to make innovation a capability with the same level of status as finance, sales, quality, or marketing. Doing this will prevent your innovation efforts from becoming a one-hit wonder.

> *For too long, innovation has been relegated to the darkest recesses of R&D departments and the conference rooms of well-meaning brainstormers. But now is the time to bring innovation to the forefront of your business.*

---

*AUTHOR'S NOTE: Over the past decade, many organizations have created an innovation capability. Dedicated innovation departments have blossomed, and a move toward solving problems (and customer needs) rather than focusing on ideas has emerged. However, innovation is often not democratized and is limited to a small group. For the average worker, the only outlet for participation in innovation is an outdated suggestion box. As you will see in the next tip, this is not a great idea.*

# 3

## ASKING FOR IDEAS IS A BAD IDEA

A large European retail bank suffering from eroding market share thought they had a great idea to solve this emerging problem. They decided to get input from all of their employees with ways to improve and grow the business. To collect employee ideas, they implemented an enterprise-wide electronic suggestion box. They believed that this would help them tap into previously undiscovered innovations. That sounds like a great idea, right? Wrong!

They received thousands of ideas. Evaluators looked at each one, and in the end, none were implemented. The company's innovation program lasted eighteen months when it was shut down and deemed a colossal failure.

In an attempt to be more innovative, many companies start by asking their employees for their ideas. This is a bad idea! The submitted ideas tend to be impractical and of low value and only create an overwhelming amount of unproductive clutter in the system.

This points to one of the most critical yet under-considered measures in the innovation process: the "signal-to-noise ratio."

The signal-to-noise ratio is an engineering term used to quantify how much a signal is corrupted by noise. For example, in an audio recording, the signal is the music, and the noise is any background hiss. A higher ratio indicates more signal than noise, which is the ultimate goal. Many online discussion forums use the term to describe the ratio between useful information and spam or false/irrelevant information.

This latter use of the term is the one that best applies to innovation.

In innovation, the signal comprises solutions that are implemented and create value. The noise consists of ideas that never come to fruition and useless suggestions for problems that don't matter and don't create value.

To increase your innovation's signal-to-noise ratio, you first want to stop asking for ideas.

Suggestion boxes are cluttered with noise, and the time required to sift through bad ideas to get to the gold is enormous. Even when you find a good suggestion, the effort needed to rally the troops to implement the idea can be significant.

In the aftermath of the bank's innovation efforts, I was asked to do a post-mortem assessment of what went wrong. In going through the submissions, I found that the ideas could be categorized into three broad groups:

DUDS: A large percentage of the ideas were not worth pursuing. They were not new or were unlikely to show a positive ROI. There might have been a nugget of usefulness among these suggestions that was missed. However, the energy to nurture these nuggets was probably not worth the effort.

FALSE NEGATIVES: These were good ideas. But for whatever reason, the evaluators dismissed them. Part of it had to do with the biases of the evaluators, and sometimes it was due to a lack of knowledge on their part. Often it was because the ideas were not fully developed, making it difficult for them to be judged appropriately.

GOOD IDEA, NO HOME: This was the most disconcerting category. The evaluators liked these ideas but had no organizational home or strategy for implementing them. As a result, the ideas withered on the vine and were never used. They never got the resources or funding necessary to move them to the next level.

The bank's experience is not unique among organizations. A well-known software company had an "idea program" that generated tens of thousands of suggestions. Less than a dozen proved to have any value, and the program was scrapped entirely.

One large retailer is known for holding a well-publicized competition each year where employees (and sometimes customers) submit new product ideas. The winner gets a large check and the company implements the best idea. I asked the person responsible for this program if it was a success. He thought about it a moment and responded, "It was a PR success but a commercial failure." The competition generated buzz in the media, but none of the products ever generated a positive return on investment.

While the company's idea-based competitions did not generate good bottom-line results, their programs focused on solving specific product improvement opportunities were a huge commercial success. The fact that this company recently stopped running its annual idea competition gives you an idea of how much value those innovative ideas brought to the company.

The other problem with asking for ideas is that there is no level of accountability. Because people tend to develop ideas on their own time, no tracking methods can keep tabs on how much energy is invested in idea generation. If you encourage ideas, you probably spend more money on those initiatives than you could imagine. You might be able to measure the ROI of a specific winning idea, but it is difficult to determine the ROI of your overall idea-based program. There is no way to know how much time was spent on the thousands of duds that never see the light of day.

My suggestion? Throw out your suggestion box!

Organizations are often enamored with collecting a large number of ideas from employees and customers. And although these can be useful for employee morale, if you go down this path, your organization needs to implement enough ideas to keep enthusiasm high. Unfortunately, the lack of traction gained by most idea platforms hurts morale and leaves the organization with a lot of extra work.

If you have infinite resources, time, and money, the idea-driven approach can help you find hidden gems.

But sometimes, the best idea is to stop asking for ideas.

 ***The signal-to-noise ratio is one of the most essential yet under-considered measures in the innovation process.***

---

*AUTHOR'S NOTE: Asking for ideas isn't always a bad idea. Most clients I work with start with an idea-driven program. It enables employees to get used to the technology being used for innovation. It also drives engagement as every employee has a suggestion on how to improve the business. Plus, it will surface ideas individuals have had but never had an outlet for sharing. However, because of the poor signal-to-noise ratio, you don't want to get stuck with the idea-driven approach as your primary strategy. After six to nine months of this approach, you want to move to the challenge-centered process outlined in the next tip.*

# 4

## DON'T THINK OUTSIDE THE BOX; FIND A BETTER BOX

L eaders of organizations often use the expression, "think outside the box" while urging their employees to innovate. The belief is that eliminating constraints and allowing people to think freely will increase creativity.

Although this Tabula Rasa or *blank slate* method to innovation is conventional wisdom, this unbounded approach actually reduces creativity and leads to abstract or impractical solutions. A television script writer in Hollywood once told me that he actually liked the idea of "creativity within constraints" as it gave him a starting point and then he could "riff" from there.

Instead of telling your employees to think outside the box, give them a "better box" to innovate inside of. These constraints will actually increase creativity and lead to useful solutions.

Albert Einstein is often quoted as saying, "If I had an hour to save the world, I would spend fifty-nine minutes defining the problem and one minute finding solutions." In my experience, most companies spend the full sixty minutes finding solutions to problems that just don't matter.

Well-defined challenges guide innovation efforts, provide useful constraints, and define that "better box."

## Challenge-Centered Innovation

All companies have challenges. They can be technical challenges on how to create a particular chemical compound. They can be marketing challenges on how to best describe your product to increase market share. They can be HR challenges around improving employee engagement. Or they can be process improvement challenges. Let's face it: your organization has no shortage of problems and you can find these challenges everywhere: from your customers, employees, shareholders, consultants, vendors, competitors, and more.

An organization's ability to change (i.e. innovate) hinges on its ability to identify and solve these challenges.

## Why Challenge-Centered Innovation?

There are a number of inherent advantages to using a challenge-centered approach over an idea-driven approach to innovation:

- Challenges are the best way to ask your employees, customers, or any community for help. It allows them to focus their energies on finding solutions that will ultimately be relevant to the needs of the organization.
- Because of the nature of challenges, there are tools to evaluate the amount of time spent finding solutions. When done properly, you can measure the ROI of each challenge and the overall challenge-centered program.
- With a challenge-centered approach, you can assign owners, resources and funding, evaluators, and evaluation criteria *before* investing the valuable time of employees and others:
- *Owner/sponsor*–In nearly every situation, a challenge has a home; someone wants this problem solved. Therefore, assign the owner of the challenge up front. This ensures

that when you get a solution, you can move things forward quickly.

- *Resources and funding*–To implement any solution, you will need people and money. Given the importance and scope of a challenge, allocate these resources up-front so that when a solution is found, you don't need to scramble.

- *Evaluators*–When solutions are submitted, you will want a team of people to evaluate the submissions. Have evaluators in place who understand the big picture and will help ensure that the best solutions are selected.

- *Evaluation criteria*–This one is important. Establish the evaluation criteria before posing the challenge, essentially creating a self-vetting process. This helps the people providing solutions know the boundaries that their solutions must meet, preventing fluffy or irrelevant answers.

The idea-driven approach to innovation does not allow for any of the above. With well-defined challenges, all of these are possible.

The difference between the idea-driven approach and the challenge-centered approach is analogous to two different fishing techniques. Idea-driven approaches are like a fisher choosing a random spot in the middle of the ocean and casting an extraordinarily expansive net. While using an untargeted approach like this might yield some fish, they will also collect shoes, tires, seaweed, and other undesirable items. And the fish they do catch are probably not the specific type they were looking for.

Contrast that with a fisher who purposefully locates a school of fish and then deliberately selects the appropriate rod, reel, line, leader, bait, and hook for catching exactly the type of fish they want, effectively minimizing waste and maximizing their efforts. As the old expression goes: "If you want to catch fish, go where the fish are." This is the challenge-centered approach.

Establishing boundaries does not necessarily put constraints on innovation efforts. In actuality, if done correctly, it has the capacity to dramatically enhance creativity and increase organizational effectiveness. So, the next time you are tempted to say "Think outside the box" - think again.

> *Albert Einstein is quoted as saying, "If I had an hour to save the world, I would spend fifty-nine minutes defining the problem and one minute finding solutions." Unfortunately, most companies spend sixty minutes finding solutions to problems that just don't matter.*

---

*AUTHOR'S NOTE: Although Einstein never said this exact quote, it is often used as shorthand for a longer quote of his: "The mere formulation of a problem is often more essential than its solution... To raise new questions, new possibilities, to regard old problems from a new angle, requires creative imagination and marks real advance in science." (from* The Evolution of Physics)

*And, because language is important, feel free to substitute "challenge" with "opportunity" or any other word that feels right. As Peter Drucker once said, "Effective people are not problem minded; they're opportunity-minded. They feed opportunities and starve problems. They think preventively."*

*An additional point to note is that it can sometimes be beneficial to avoid sharing evaluation criteria with solvers as this information might cause them to prematurely filter their ideas. This is particularly true for scientists and engineers who tend to seek the one "correct" answer. In some situations, presenting the problem reframed in various ways can stimulate their thinking more effectively. The optimal strategy depends on the situation and the nature of the solvers. For instance, when using crowdsourcing, encouraging such self-filtering could be advantageous to minimize the submission of irrelevant solutions.*

## 5

---

## EXPERTISE IS THE ENEMY OF INNOVATION

U nilever, the giant consumer goods company, wanted to develop a toothpaste that would whiten teeth without using the traditional methods of bleach or abrasives. The toothpaste experts didn't have a solution. Recognizing the limitations of their own knowledge, they asked themselves, "Who else makes whites whiter?" They quickly realized that a different Unilever business unit made laundry detergents that whiten clothes without bleach. They learned that most detergents use a bluing agent to make whites *appear* whiter. With this information, they created their "Signal White Now" (and other brands) toothpaste. Instead of harsh bleaches and abrasives, the toothpaste has a blue dye that runs through the middle, creating the immediate optical illusion of white teeth. Toothpaste experts were seemingly unable to solve this problem on their own. This breakthrough solution was discovered only when people with different specializations were brought together.

While this might seem surprising, this is not uncommon. Expertise can indeed be the enemy of breakthrough thinking. The more you know about a particular topic, the more difficult it is to think about it differently. Your solutions will most likely be "been there, done that" ideas limited to your area of expertise. If you want breakthroughs, you must bring together people from various disciplines, backgrounds, and experiences.

This idea was confirmed by research completed by Lee Fleming, a business administration professor at Harvard Business School. After analyzing 17,000 patents, he discovered that the breakthroughs that arise from multidisciplinary work "are frequently of unusually high value–superior to the best innovations achieved by conventional approaches."

His research highlighted the pros and cons of each method. He learned that teams composed of people with similar backgrounds have many successes yet yield fewer breakthroughs. On the other hand, cross-disciplinary teams had a higher failure rate, yet their innovations were more radical and had the potential to create incredible value.

Is there a way to get all the benefits of diversity without any adverse effects?

Yes. It is called "open innovation."

Open innovation is an innovation process where you engage people outside your organization to help solve challenges. One common form of open innovation occurs when you post your challenges on a website and get responses from a diverse group of outside experts. Many organizations find this tool helpful in speeding up the innovation process because it taps into specializations that might not exist within your organization.

A widely publicized open innovation competition was the "Netflix Prize." Netflix wanted to improve the quality of its video recommendation engine by 10 percent. This was valued as being worth millions of dollars in additional revenue. Instead of trying to improve the algorithm in-house, they decided to award one-million-dollars to the first person or team who could find a good solution. Although it took three years, a seven-person team of "statisticians, machine-learning experts, and computer engineers" from the United States, Austria, Canada, and Israel developed an algorithm that improved recommendations by 10.06 percent, resulting in their being awarded the prize money. For Netflix, this was a bargain. It would have cost them much more money to develop the solution internally, and who knows if they would have found one.

Here's how it works: You post a challenge to your website or an intermediary's website. After a short period of time, you will receive anywhere from dozens to hundreds of solutions, although quite a bit less than you would receive using idea-driven innovation. Although some won't be useful, all you need is one solution that does work. And with some forms of open innovation, you only pay for the solutions that work. But the real advantage is that people from many disciplines can chime in with various solutions, increasing the likelihood of a breakthrough. When open innovation is done correctly, you won't be overloaded with useless submissions.

Remember the BP oil spill that was discussed earlier? They received 123,000 ideas. Contrast that with how open innovation was applied to another oil spill–the Exxon Valdez disaster in Alaska.

In 1989, the Exxon Valdez tanker crashed into a reef in Prince William Sound in Alaska, dumping 10.8 million gallons of crude oil into the water. Although some of the oil was recovered, a large amount remained trapped under the ice. When teams tried to move the oil, the water/oil mixture froze. Oil engineers worked on this challenge for twenty years without any viable solution until they discovered open innovation. They posted a well-formed challenge to the website of an intermediary, InnoCentive (now part of Wazoku), a company with an extensive network of experts from a wide range of disciplines who solve complex problems for a monetary prize.

A solution to the oil crisis was found very quickly. Interestingly, the winning solution did not come from the oil industry. Instead, it came from someone in the construction industry who had a similar challenge with pouring wet cement; he needed to find a way to prevent it from hardening immediately. This chemist developed a device that vibrates the molecules so that they flow continuously. He figured that if vibrating could keep the cement from hardening, a similar concept could be adapted to keep the oil in the tanks from freezing. Bringing together diverse disciplines through an open innovation platform solved this decades-old problem.

Another great example comes from NASA. Solar activity is a significant problem for space travel and can be incredibly dangerous for astronauts. For decades, NASA has been unsuccessful in finding a model that would allow them to predict solar activity with a high level of accuracy.

To find a solution, they turned to open innovation. Their success criteria for the solution was that the model would need to provide a prediction within twenty-four hours of the solar activity, it needed to be 50 percent accurate, and within two sigma (a quality measure where the higher the number, the better). The best solution predicted activity within eight hours was 70 percent accurate and within three sigma. This was a vast improvement over NASA's initial expectations. Who had the solution? A retired engineer who studied dropped cell phone calls and, in the process, discovered a predictive model for solar flares.

Sometimes the best solutions come from outside your area of expertise and beyond the four walls of your organization. By the end, you might find solutions to problems that have stumped the experts for years.

 *If you are NASA and have one hundred aerospace engineers working on an aerospace engineering challenge, adding the 101st aerospace engineer may not help that much. But adding a physicist, a nanotechnologist, a chemist, a biologist, or even a musician may move your solutions in a completely new direction.*

*AUTHOR'S NOTE: I have always been fascinated with the innovation resulting from collaboration across industries and disciplines. In 2009, this was the topic of my TEDxNASA speech to nearly 2,000 aerospace engineers. The title was "Rocket Science Isn't Always Rocket Science." It is a brief six minutes, and I think you will enjoy it. You can watch it here: www.ShapiroTEDx.com*

# PROCESS

## CHALLENGE-CENTERED INNOVATION

Efficient innovation requires an efficient innovation process. When done correctly, the innovation process starts with a challenge and ends with value creation. Unfortunately, the process used by most organizations is unfocused and creates unnecessary work. This section explores various aspects of the innovation process: challenges, competition, collaboration, and crowdsourcing. Your innovation efforts will be more focused and efficient by using a combination of these strategies.

# 6

## THE DIFFERENCE BETWEEN A PIPELINE AND A SEWER IS WHAT FLOWS THROUGH IT

W e hear the expression "innovation pipeline" tossed around a lot. But if you aren't careful, your pipeline may get clogged.

The biggest challenge companies face is to figure out which challenges to solve. I call this their "meta-challenge." Given that organizations have limited resources and money, prioritization is critical.

Several well-known companies have invested poorly in innovation, resulting in disaster. Although Blockbuster Inc., the national video rental chain, was constantly innovating, they never innovated where they needed it most: their business model. As a result, they invested a lot of energy yet went nowhere quickly, eventually landing in bankruptcy. Likewise, Xerox's fabled Palo Alto Research Center (PARC) was always focused on radical and game-changing innovations, yet they never found ways to bring their inventions to market. Apple was the ultimate beneficiary of Xerox PARC's hard work.

You want to manage your innovation pipeline like your personal investment portfolio. Putting all your money in a savings account, making 1 percent interest, may be safe, but your investment will never grow, and you will most likely end up destitute. Then again, putting all your money in risky derivatives and speculative investments with an enormous potential upside also has an equally significant downside and will most likely land you in the gutter. The buzzword in the finance world is diversification.

**Your Innovation Portfolio**

Equally, your innovation portfolio should comprise a diverse set of investments in various challenges. Include some safe bets (incremental innovation) and riskier investments (radical innovation). It's up to you to decide the correct proportion of each one. You want a variety of challenges, ranging from service to product-enhancement challenges and performance improvement to business-model-changing challenges.

Challenges tend to fall into two broad categories: technical challenges (e.g., how can we create a new chemical compound with specific properties?) and marketing challenges (e.g., how can we get women to drink beer rather than wine?).

When you map these two dimensions, you get the following chart with four broad categories of challenges:

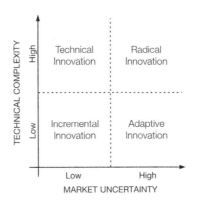

- INCREMENTAL INNOVATION: This is the portfolio
  equivalent of investing in CDs and Money Markets.
  These are safe and yield returns. This is where the lion's
  share of innovation money is invested, as it should be.
  But don't put all of your eggs in this basket. Too many
  safe bets, in the long run, are unsafe. Generally, these
  innovations are both technically easy and have a clear
  customer benefit. For example, the next generation of
  your product or service would often fall into this
  category.
- ADAPTIVE INNOVATION: These challenges are easy to
  implement from a technical perspective but represent a
  departure from a known market need. As a result, you
  don't know if consumers will be interested or how to get
  them interested. For example, when Chrysler
  introduced the minivan, it was an incremental technical
  effort but presented a complex marketing challenge
  since nothing like it previously existed. In other cases,
  innovation is about adapting an old product and
  bringing it to a new market. For example, a razor blade
  company wanted to find ways to get teenage boys to
  shave more often. Experimentation and sophisticated
  market research are often the answer to these
  challenges.
- TECHNICAL INNOVATION: This category deals with any
  innovation that serves a well-established need yet is
  technically complex to develop. The obvious example is
  finding a better cure for a disease. Still, other examples
  might include NASA's need for predictive modeling of
  solar flare activity or creating a razor blade made of
  plastic with the strength of steel. As you will discover,
  open innovation (described in the previous tip) is an
  extremely useful technique for finding solutions to
  technically complex challenges.

- RADICAL INNOVATION: These innovations are both technically complex and have high market uncertainty. The Sony Walkman (now retired) is a well-worn example of this. Apple's integration of iTunes with the iPod could fall into this category as the "technically" difficult part was getting all artists and recording studios to agree to allow digital music to be sold. These challenges are the riskiest as they can be costly with a lower likelihood of success. But when successful, these innovations can be game-changing.

It is not important to debate where specific challenges might fall. For example, you could argue that the iPod/iTunes met a known market need since consumers were already downloading digital music from Napster, albeit without paying. The key is ensuring you balance the different types of challenges. This can help you hedge your bets.

In Lewis Carroll's "Through the Looking-Glass," the Red Queen said, "It takes all the running you can do, to keep in the same place." Only investing in incremental innovation results in hard work with little progress. On the other hand, always swinging for the fences will have you striking out most of the time. Diversify your innovation portfolio, and you will keep your pipeline flowing smoothly.

 *Too many safe bets, in the long run, are unsafe.*

---

*AUTHOR'S NOTE: I can't take credit for the "innovation sewer" expression. This was given to me during a lunchtime conversation with a pharmaceutical client. At the time, they lacked clarity on where to invest, resulting in a struggle to grow the business. Since then, they got focused* and produced some blockbuster drugs, which has made them one of the most valuable pharmaceutical companies.

On a related note, as is the case with all innovation, what was a breakthrough in the past may become irrelevant. Just as the Walkman has long since been retired, so has the iPod. Now that the iPhone allows you to carry all of your music in your pocket without an extra device, the iPod no longer serves a vital function.

# 7

## THE GOLDILOCKS PRINCIPLE

R emember the story of Goldilocks? She enters the house of three bears. After sampling their porridge, she decides to go to sleep. She finds the papa bear's bed too hard, the mama bear's bed too soft, and the baby bear's bed just right. The same is true when defining challenges. They can't be too big (broad or abstract, e.g., asking for new ideas) or too small (overly specific, e.g., extremely technical that can only be solved by one discipline). They must be "just right"–framed to maximize the likelihood of finding a workable solution.

When framing challenges, you must adhere to the Goldilocks Principle.

TOO BIG
Broad and Abstract

JUST RIGHT
Maximum Likelihood
of Being Solved

TOO SMALL
Overly Specific
and Single Discipline

It is common for a company to ask its employees to find ways to increase revenue. This is a lofty goal, and posing this type of general challenge usually results in fluffy solutions. Instead of asking people to solve broad problems, ask specific questions that will likely result in an implementable solution. For example, are there specific markets that you have not yet penetrated? Are you missing out on customer segments that present a greater opportunity?

When a cell phone company wanted to improve customer service, instead of simply asking people how to improve the customer experience, they analyzed call data and found ten primary reasons people dialed into the call center. One of the most common reasons was a specific billing issue. The solution? It was concluded that the best way to improve customer service in the call center had nothing to do with the call center itself. Instead, it involved changing the tariffs associated with this particular issue. This one small change resulted in dramatically reduced call volumes and higher customer satisfaction. The only way that this solution could have been found was by asking a more specific question backed up by data.

Or consider a not-for-profit organization that wanted to

improve the education system of England. Another lofty goal indeed, and had they asked people for solutions to such a significant problem, the answers would have been all over the map. Instead, they did their research. They discovered that the greatest factor in a child's education was not the education system itself but rather parental involvement. Therefore, the challenge became how to increase parental involvement in a child's education, particularly in urban, disadvantaged communities. The data and research they had collected provided deeper insights. The solutions were more focused, practical, and valuable than they would have been had the question been more generally focused on the entire education system. The winning solution was based on work done at an experimental school in Bogotá, Colombia, where parental involvement reached nearly 100 percent and student learning skyrocketed. A solution found halfway around the world now had the potential to change the educational outcomes of students in the UK.

NASA has had great success with open innovation. They have found solutions to problems that have plagued space travel for decades. One challenge was designed to find a "microgravity laundry system." The solutions they received were not as practical as they had hoped. In hindsight, they recognized two crucial lessons.

First, they realized that asking a "system" question might have been too complex, and the larger challenge might have been more effectively solved by deconstructing it into a series of smaller challenges (e.g., a valve challenge).

Second, the potentially more important lesson was that they may have been better served by asking an even higher-level question. That is, asking about a laundry system implied that the solution was mechanical in nature. However, they might have found more interesting solutions had they asked how to eliminate the need for clothes laundering altogether. This might have led to an entirely different breakthrough. So, in this case, you could argue that the original challenge was too narrowly defined.

The previously discussed Exxon Valdez oil spill provides another example of a challenge being initially too narrowly defined. When the "freezing" problem was posed as an oil challenge, only oil experts worked on the problem. When the challenge was posed as a "viscous shearing" issue, the problem was no longer about oil (a specific fluid) but rather a common problem in fluid dynamics. When the challenge was phrased this way, it allowed for solutions from various disciplines, including the construction industry, where the fix was eventually found.

A critical step in finding solutions is clearly defining the challenge. The way a challenge is framed will impact the way it is solved.

Some may suggest that Goldilocks's decision to enter the home belonging to the three bears in the woods was not very sound. However, it was her quest for "just right" that allowed her to rest peacefully. If you adopt this same rigor when defining your challenges, you too might sleep better at night, knowing a workable solution is just around the corner.

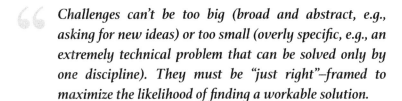

*Challenges can't be too big (broad and abstract, e.g., asking for new ideas) or too small (overly specific, e.g., an extremely technical problem that can be solved only by one discipline). They must be "just right"–framed to maximize the likelihood of finding a workable solution.*

---

AUTHOR'S NOTE: *I discuss the Goldilocks Principle extensively in* Invisible Solutions. *That book includes twenty-five lenses that help you reframe a problem or opportunity. Ten of them are specifically dedicated to increasing or decreasing the level of abstraction and are designed to help you find reframes that are "just right." One lens is the RESULT lens which asks, "What does this make possible?" In other words, get clear on the result of solving the problem and solve for that. You can use the*

*RESULT lens by adding two words to the end of your existing problem: "so that." For example, with the education system from above, "We have an education system so that..." In this case, the answer was "so that children can learn necessary skills." These two words help you focus on the end game rather than the means.*

# 8

# THERE IS NO SUCH THING AS A "KNOW-IT-ALL"

Recently, a well-known healthcare company faced a tricky challenge. After launching an incredibly successful new product, they focused on creating new complementary offerings. Multiple failed attempts later, they realized they didn't have the in-house expertise to crack the code. Not knowing what to do, they decided to try posting the challenge on an open innovation website. They hoped they could find someone outside their organization who could find a practical solution.

Unfortunately, some employees took this action as a slap in the face. Unfamiliar with the benefits of open innovation, they felt that someone within the organization could solve every challenge. To prove their point, several employees took it upon themselves to submit solutions to the posted challenge.

In the end, the solutions submitted by the employees weren't chosen. The breakthrough answer came from someone not only outside of the company but outside of the company's industry. The successful conclusion of this challenge solidified the company's decision to formally launch its open innovation efforts. Their conclusion?

No one person can solve every problem.

And its corollary:

No one organization can solve every problem.

The late great Will Rogers once said, "There is nothing so stupid as an educated man if you get him off the thing that he was educated in."

One of the challenges with driving innovation in organizations is that smart people are often more interested in being right than doing right. That is, they want to believe that they can solve every problem under the sun. This pervasive belief can circumvent your innovation efforts.

To be clear, the objective of open innovation is not to replace the smarts you already have in your organization. It is to augment this brilliance. Most companies don't have enough time to solve all the challenges they are working on. Unfortunately, R&D people often get spread too thin working on many different types of challenges, some of which could be better solved by others outside the company.

Here's a simple model I use to help companies determine which challenges should be solved externally versus those that can be solved internally.

Broadly speaking, challenges fall into roughly three categories:

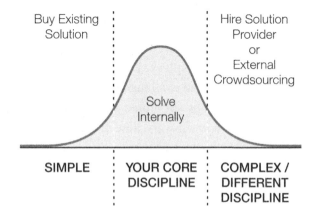

SIMPLE CHALLENGES: On the left-hand side of the bell curve, you have the challenges where there is a high probability that someone else has already solved this specific problem. Although you could solve them internally, this is not the best use of your resources. The odds are that someone else already has a solution you could buy or license for less money in less time. Why waste your highly specialized experts on these types of challenges?

- *Buying an Existing Solution*: For these types of challenges, tech scouting (as an example) is a great way to procure existing solutions by scanning patent databases and other technology repositories. You can then license or purchase the technology for your own use. With this strategy, you are buying a solution from a single provider.

COMPLEX OR UNSOLVED CHALLENGES: On the right-hand side of the bell curve, you have exceptionally complex challenges that may have remained unsolved within your organization for years. Or maybe it is viewed as being outside your area of expertise. For example, because space travel can last for years, NASA has a problem with food spoilage. Over the years, they have tried different packaging materials with no success. Even people from the food packaging industry could not find a solution. With nowhere else to turn, they decided to run an open innovation challenge. The solution they found came from someone in Russia with no food experience. He developed a graphite-based material that keeps food fresher longer than regular materials.

In general, for these complex challenges, there are two primary strategies for finding solutions: 1) Hiring a solution provider or 2) Crowdsourcing a solution.

- *Hiring a Solution Provider:* A third party takes ownership of delivering the result and can solve (and potentially implement) some challenges. You might choose to work with a university or issue a "Request for Proposal" to find a solution provider. Regardless, in these situations, you aren't buying a solution as much as you're selecting an outsourcing partner. These alliances are best used for complex challenges that can't be deconstructed into smaller ones or where deep context knowledge is required.

- *Crowdsourcing a Solution:* Posting your problem to "the world" and allowing a few weeks or months for someone to submit a workable solution is the best solution to other challenges. Then you can buy or license the solution. The difference between this and the previous approach is here; you are purchasing a solution, not a solution provider. Crowdsourcing is great for technically complex challenges that can be defined at the right level of granularity, like the NASA food spoilage challenge.

CHALLENGES WITHIN YOUR DISCIPLINE: In the middle of the bell curve are the challenges that fall into your organization's sweet spot. These are the challenges that your experts are best equipped to solve. By "outsourcing" the simple and complex/unsolved challenges, you can allow your team to focus on what they do best. This will increase your ability to solve the problems that differentiate you from your competition. Although there are several methods for finding solutions internally, here are the two most common approaches:

- *Internal Individual/Team:* This is the most common way challenges are solved. You use internal people whose job is to solve these types of challenges. For example, this would include members of the development team assigned to a particular product. The solutions may come from brainstorming or through a deep technical understanding of the problem. This method is preferred when deep contextual knowledge is required and would be difficult to transfer elsewhere. It is an excellent place to start for solving many types of challenges.

- *Internal Crowdsourcing:* Sometimes, people inside your organization who are not assigned to the given problem find the best solutions. It might be a customer service representative who finds a great new branding solution or a researcher in a different part of the organization who solves a technical challenge. These solutions are typically found by posting the challenge on your intranet or a platform specifically designed for this purpose. This generally is an excellent place to turn next when the dedicated team can't find an answer.

They say there is more than one way to skin a cat. And there is more than one way to solve a challenge. Although some challenges are solved in a moment of genius, most require a more formal thought process. The key to efficient innovation is determining which mechanism would best yield a viable solution for that specific challenge.

The approaches listed above represent only a few of the possible strategies. If one technique (e.g., internal team) does not yield a workable solution, try a different approach (e.g., external crowdsourcing). People want to be (and should be) appreciated for their brilliance. They have dedicated their lives to the pursuit of knowledge. But everyone cannot be educated in everything. Figure out what you (and your organization) do best, and find others to help with everything else.

Or, to quote Will Rogers again, "Everybody is ignorant. Only on different subjects."

 *"There is nothing so stupid as an educated man if you get him off the thing that he was educated in." —Will Rogers.*

---

*AUTHOR'S NOTE: Over the past decade, open innovation has evolved significantly. Some providers focus on creating ecosystems and partner networks. That's currently the in-vogue concept. Others have improved our ability to find existing solutions quickly. And AI is rapidly changing the game for solution-finding. Regardless, the principles remain the same. And as this book is focused on principles rather than technologies or specific solutions, I would encourage you to do some research on this topic, as it is ever-changing.*

*In the context of Generative AI, the concept of "a better box" is arguably more critical than ever. The "prompts" used to query the bot largely determine the quality of the generated solutions. Broad prompts tend to produce generic solutions, while overly specific ones can result in narrow answers, leading to a potential miss of the broader context and associated valuable information. Much like humans, computers need the right questions to derive the best solutions.*

# 9

# WHAT DID EDISON GET WRONG ABOUT INNOVATION?

W hile attempting to find a suitable filament to make the incandescent electric light a viable device, Edison is famous for saying, "I have not failed 700 times. I have not failed once. I have succeeded in proving that those 700 ways will not work. When I have eliminated the ways that will not work, I will find the way that will work."

Depending on the source, Edison tried 700, 1,000, or 10,000 different filaments in his attempt to improve the light bulb.

Regardless of which number is accurate, innovators around the world continue to embrace this quote because it seems to validate the iterative development process used by so many. There is a widely held belief that you should keep trying and failing until you find a solution that works because you learn as much from failure as you do from success.

Regardless, each of Edison's 700 attempts cost him time and money.

If Edison had found a solution to the light bulb challenge on the first try, would he have continued to seek out 700 other ways that did not work? Did finding ways that did not work really add that much value? Can your organization afford 700 unsuccessful attempts? Not in today's competitive environment.

Think about it this way...

### ITERATIVE DEVELOPMENT

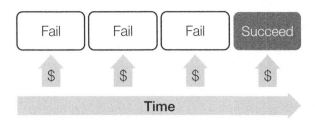

Look at the chart above. With the traditional model, you fail repeatedly until you are finally successful. Because your employees work and invest their time in each attempt, it costs the organization payroll and overhead. And because the failure process happens serially, it takes a long time. Of course, if you are successful on the first attempt, life is good. But that rarely happens in the real world.

Unfortunately, the reality is that failure is often a necessary part of innovation. We can never instantly know the solution to a problem until we test it out via experimentation (see tip 24). But is there a better way to find solutions that minimize your risk, cost, and time – especially for technical challenges?

# MASSIVE PARALLEL PROCESS

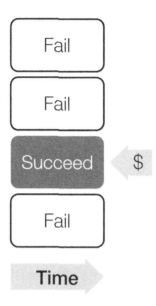

The chart above is based on a challenge-centered, open innovation model. Alph Bingham, founder of InnoCentive, describes challenge-centered open innovation as a "massively parallel process where failures and successes happen at the same time." With this approach, you have the same number of failures, but there are two differences. One: The failures are happening in parallel rather than in a series, significantly speeding up your time to solution. Two: The cost of failure is pushed into the market, and you only pay for the value received instead of paying for the time invested. That is, you only pay for a successful solution.

Say you post a challenge and you get dozens (or hundreds) of people working to find solutions. Some solutions won't work, but all you need is one that does work, and with this form of open innovation, you only pay for successful outcomes. Failures cost you nothing in terms of time and money. With internal iterative development, you pay for the successes and the failures.

Do you really learn enough from your failures to justify the extra cost and time involved? Probably not.

What should you do to take advantage of this massive parallel process?

For technically complex challenges (as opposed to challenges with market uncertainty which are typically best developed via experimentation), find ways of avoiding internal experimentation and identify others who can share the risk. Look for developers willing to be paid based on results rather than time invested. The objective is to move away from the fixed costs associated with your internal development efforts and move towards a variable model where you pay only for the value of the solutions you need.

Edison was a great inventor. And I suspect that if Edison were alive today, given the tools available, he might have tried an entirely different approach to developing the sustainable filament.

 *Challenge-centered, open innovation is a "massively parallel process where failures and successes happen at the same time."—Alph Bingham, founder of InnoCentive.*

---

*AUTHOR'S NOTE: I am a fan of open innovation and the massive parallel process associated with it. I encourage my clients to consider the concepts in this tip and the previous one. Employees within a company can not solve every problem. And even if they could, it might cost you too much time and money. What if you looked externally for solutions to many of your challenges instead? The next tip provides some thoughts on how to run external crowdsourcing challenges most effectively.*

## 10

---

# WHAT DO CISCO, LG ELECTRONICS, AND GE HAVE IN COMMON WITH AMERICAN IDOL?

E ven after all these years, *American Idol* remains one of the most popular television shows. Why? Partly because it is entertaining and partially because the show can uncover previously undiscovered talent.

It is this latter reason why many organizations are employing the *American Idol* approach to innovation. Their objective is to uncover some truly amazing ideas or previously hidden solutions.

## Innovation Tournaments

In the innovation space, these events are sometimes called "innovation tournaments," a term coined by Christian Terwiesch and Karl Ulrich from Stanford University in their book *Innovation Tournaments*.

The NCAA basketball championships are a tournament. The World Series of Poker is a tournament. Television's *Survivor*, *The Amazing Race*, and *Big Brother* are all tournaments. What makes each of these a tournament? Quite simply, there is always a winner, although it is not necessarily winner-takes-all.

Cisco, LG Electronics, and GE have all used the "find a winner" model to develop ideas.

The Cisco iPrize was a tournament they ran in 2010. When it was announced, the company said they would "select up to thirty-two semifinalist teams that will work with Cisco experts to build a business plan and presentation... Up to eight finalist teams will present their business ideas to a judging panel to compete for the grand prize: a $250,000 award shared equally by members of the winning team." In the end, there were a total of 2,900 participants who submitted 824 ideas. Ideas were, as planned, narrowed down to thirty-two semifinalist ideas, with nine teams reaching the tournament's final phase. The winning team did indeed receive $250,000.

LG Electronics held a similar tournament in 2009 and 2010. They wanted people to "design their version of the next revolutionary LG mobile phone." A total of more than eighty thousand dollars in awards was given out, with the winner receiving twenty thousand dollars. The tournament had 835 submissions from 324 individuals. They shared with me that about 75 percent of the ideas were things they had previously thought of; only 25 percent had innovative elements. The process was similar to the Cisco iPrize approach: Judges reviewed all eight hundred plus concepts and narrowed them down to the top one hundred for round-two judges to review. Round-three judges only reviewed the top forty-three concepts.

GE used a similar approach for its "Ecomagination" challenges.

The common link between these tournaments is that there would always be a winner. Just like *American Idol* and other tournaments, once they got through the duds, each organization had semi-finalists, finalists, and the ultimate winner. But just because someone "wins" does not mean their talent or idea is good or useful.

## Bounty Hunting

When is an innovation tournament not a tournament? And when is a tournament not the right approach?

A tournament fails when you are not interested in simply finding the "best" submission but rather finding the "right" solution. That is, you don't want to crown a winner for the sake of naming a champion. Instead, the objective is to find workable solutions to a real and specific business problem.

Think of these as contingency-based, value-priced challenges. Admittedly, that does not sound as sexy as calling it an "innovation tournament."

Here's how it works: A company wants a problem solved, so they decide the "value" of finding a workable solution and offer a "bounty" to anyone who can provide one. The bounty is only paid when they get what they need. This "pay for solution" model outsources the risk associated with complex problem-solving.

The two most well-known approaches to innovation bounties were the Netflix Prize and the X Prize.

In the case of Netflix (described in tip 5), they only paid the team that ultimately improved the recommendation engine by 10 percent. Netflix wasn't looking for the best solution; they were looking for one that met their specific needs. The bounty-based approach was useful because they only paid one million dollars when they received a successful solution.

The Ansari X Prize was a space competition in which twenty-six teams competed for a ten-million-dollar prize, which would be awarded to the first non-government organization to "build and launch a spacecraft capable of carrying three people to one hundred kilometers above the Earth's surface, twice within two weeks." As with the Netflix Prize, the bounty was only paid out when the X Prize's specific criteria were met. Interestingly, although ten million dollars was awarded to the winning Tier One project's space plane, *SpaceShipOne*, it is reported that more than one hundred million dollars was invested in new technologies in pursuit of the prize.

## Tournament Versus Bounty

The key difference is how these challenges were articulated. The success criteria are clearly defined with the bounty-based approach: Did you improve the recommendation engine by 10 percent? Did you find a chemical compound that has specific properties? Did you develop a mathematical model that optimizes a specific problem? The "winner" of the bounty is determined by the given criteria. If the criteria are not met, the bounty is not paid.

With the tournament-based approach, the success criteria are often not well defined. The winner is the "best" of the submissions. Although these competitions can yield excellent solutions, I know from inside information that the results are often less than stellar.

Tournaments are great for getting a broad set of ideas in an undefined space. And they are handy for things like the Pepsi Refresh Project, that are designed to generate a lot of buzz. Bounties, on the other hand, are great for hunting down practical solutions. Use these when you want the best solution, just not the best of the bunch. However, both approaches can provide value to any organization when used correctly.

*With the bounty-based approach, the success criteria are clearly defined. With the tournament-based approach, the winner is the "best" of the submissions.*

*AUTHOR'S NOTE: This tip mirrors the content from tips 3 and 4, where I describe idea-driven innovation versus challenge-centered innovation. The* American Idol *approach is analogous to the idea-driven approach and is about quantity and finding hidden gems. You have to sort through a ton of terrible singers to find the big star. The bounty-based approach is like challenge-centered innovation.* You know precisely what you want and the selection criteria, and you will reject any solution that doesn't meet your needs. In Invisible Solutions, I go into greater depth about idea-driven and challenge-centered innovation. To be clear, there is potential for incredible value with both approaches. In fact, in 2015, GE published, "Now ten years old, Ecomagination has generated more than $200 billion in revenues since inception." This is a great example of a well-run tournament designed to generate real impact.

# 11

## TO COMPETE OR NOT COMPETE: THAT IS THE QUESTION

Open-source software is a well-known collaborative community. Many developers participate solely to be part of the community, contribute to the greater good, and build on each other's solutions. On the other hand, developers who work on creating apps for the iPhone operate in a competitive marketplace. Their contribution is primarily, although not always, driven by a financial return, and they tend to work independently.

As we saw in the previous tip, innovation tournaments, and bounties can be run competitively or collaboratively. Cisco and LG Electronics ran competitive tournaments so no one could see the rival submissions. On the other hand, GE ran their Ecomagination challenges collaboratively, allowing anyone to comment on or vote for any submission. The Netflix Prize and X Prize (both innovation bounties) were run as competitions yet allowed for collaboration within each submission.

This raises an important question. Which approach yields better solutions: competition or collaboration?

Kevin Boudreau and Karim Lakhani wrote an article on this topic in the *MIT Sloane Management Review* that examined the merits of each form of open innovation. They found collaboration useful when problems require "cumulative knowledge" and involve "building on past advances." On the other hand, competition is most effective when "an innovation problem is solved by broad experimentation."

They also found that collaborative "communities often are more oriented toward the intrinsic motivations of external innovators, whereas (competitive) markets tend to reward extrinsic motivation."

For your corporate innovation efforts, should you use competition or collaboration?

The answer is you should use both. In fact, you may want to use both approaches for a single challenge. However, it is important to go about it in the correct sequence.

Let's first address a few psychological issues related to creative thinking.

Think about your typical group brainstorming session. Although this is a common way for organizations to innovate, is this approach effective? Interestingly, research suggests that individuals working on their own produce a higher quality and quantity of ideas than when they work collaboratively. There are several reasons for this:

- *Serial Processing:* If you have ten individuals in a group, only one can speak at any given time. This limits the "bandwidth" of ideas that can be processed. Ten people working individually could theoretically generate ten times more ideas at the same time. However, collaboration tools can eliminate this problem as people can work in unison, allowing everyone to "speak" simultaneously. IBM's Jam events are a popular way to get groups of people to create concurrently.
- *Social Loafing:* When groups work together, there is a tendency for individuals to put forth less effort. They assume that someone else will pick up the slack. Although this is true for group brainstorming sessions,

this factor tends to have a reduced impact when using other forms of innovation (such as open innovation).

- *Groupthink:* Finally, it has been shown that if you start the process by working together, you end up with groupthink. That is, as soon as the first idea is thrown out, it tends to influence the thinking of the other contributors. This causes a convergence of solutions too early in the process and narrows the set of ideas that are typically generated.

It is this last reason why starting the process - whether you are using face-to-face brainstorming or virtual crowdsourcing - through a "competitive" approach to problem-solving is good. When conducting brainstorming sessions, it works best to have each person write down their creative ideas independently. Only after everyone generates their own list does the group come together. When using a crowdsourcing approach, it is often helpful to start with a competition to get the broadest range of solutions, and then, only after selecting the best solutions do you allow a collaborative community to flesh them out. This gives you a much richer solution in the end.

Several years ago, I wanted a new logo for my website and decided to crowdsource a design using 99designs.com. After posting a "brief" describing what I wanted, I had a choice: use a collaborative or competitive approach. With the collaborative model, every designer could see the submissions of the other contributors along with my comments on the designs. With the competitive approach, I could use blind submissions where the designers couldn't see anyone else's work. I chose the collaborative design approach. Initially, the designs trickled in slowly; many designers sat back and waited until there seemed to be a convergence around one idea. The variety of designs was relatively low.

I used a different approach when it came time to design the cards for my fourth book, *Personality Poker.* I first used the competitive model (i.e., blind submissions). I found a much greater variety of submissions right from the start, but there was no opportunity for people to build on the ideas of others. Therefore, I followed up with a collaborative challenge after running the competition. This process yielded a wide choice of initial designs followed by a high level of collaborative refinement. The final result was better than anything a single designer could have developed.

The most successful model, from this experience, was competition followed by collaboration.

Of course, other factors will influence your use of a competitive versus collaborative approach. For example, if intellectual property issues are critical, blind competitions work better since they provide greater protection for the designers. However, even in that situation, you can have groups work together to submit a competitive solution. Or, when allocating prizes (monetary or other), competitions are easier to manage as submissions are clearly delineated. But even with collaborative solutions, creative ways of divvying up the winnings exist. It does not need to be winner takes all.

For social issues about the public good, collaboration often works well because you can take the pulse of a variety of people. Don't fall into the trap of believing that public opinion will lead you to the right solution (see the next tip).

Every situation is different, and it is up to you to figure out which approach will work best for your particular challenge.

*Collaboration and competition both serve an essential purpose in the innovation process. As Alexander Graham Bell once said, "Great discoveries and improvements invariably involve the cooperation of many minds. I may be given credit for having blazed the trail, but when I look at the subsequent developments, I feel the credit is due to others rather than to myself."*

---

*AUTHOR'S NOTE: This tip was based on an article I wrote titled "Brainstorming is Stupid." You can see a theme here. The point of the article was that we need to change how to conduct these types of meetings. The first step is to ensure you have a diverse group of individuals in the room (see tips 5 and 26). Then ensure you have a well-framed challenge (see tips 4 and 6). Now you are ready to find solutions. Ask everyone to write down their own perspectives. Next, have them share with one other person. Then they share at their table (typically four to eight people). Finally, each table shares with the entire room. This process gets the broadest range of perspectives and allows even the most introverted person to have a voice.*

# 12

# BE SURE TO AVOID MOBSOURCING

I magine you are the former Governor of California, Arnold Schwarzenegger. Your state is struggling with myriad issues ranging from a perpetual and growing deficit to a decaying education system to an infrastructure that can't handle the ever-increasing population.

What do you do?

Like any good innovator, you would turn to crowdsourcing, just as Governor Schwarzenegger did. He created a Twitter-based (now "X") site called MyIdea4CA.com, which allows anyone to post their suggestions and comments and vote on the best ideas. Thousands of people participated. Which idea (at one time) received the greatest support?

Did it involve reducing government spending? Did it help improve traffic and other infrastructure issues? Did it tackle educational issues? No. The winning idea was...

Legalize and tax marijuana.

Although the crowds felt that this might be the best way to solve many of the state's woes, it didn't solve any of the problems that the government wanted to handle.

In August 2009, a *New York Times* story detailed a similar effort by President Barack Obama to elicit ideas from the American public.

"The White House made its first major entree into government by the people last month when it set up an online forum to ask ordinary people for their ideas on carrying out the president's open-government pledge. It got an earful–on legalizing marijuana, revealing UFO secrets, and verifying Mr. Obama's birth certificate to prove he was really born in the United States and thus eligible to be president."

Asking people for their opinions and allowing them to vote is not always the best way to run your innovation efforts.

What can we learn from all of this?

First and foremost, as stated in a previous tip, it is critical to define the challenge clearly. Both of these platforms were built around broad and ambiguous questions. Also, because of its Twitter-based platform, the MyIdea4CA site only allowed submissions that were less than 140 characters. In such a limited space, it's hard to get into a meaty discussion, let alone provide deep and thoughtful solutions.

But there is another important lesson here.

Crowdsourcing is not intended to be a democratic tool designed to gather the whims and wishes of individuals. It is intended to source solutions, not opinions.

Some might refer to what we see on these sites as mobsourcing. This occurs when a few people lead the pack and provide most of the input while the rest of the crowd hops on the bandwagon without adding anything meaningful to the discussion.

This explains why voting is not usually the most effective way of sorting through ideas, suggestions, or solutions. Have you ever tried using a democratic voting mechanism to whittle down a long list of submissions? If so, how effective was it? I suspect it probably didn't work out as nicely as you had hoped. There are four primary reasons for this:

- Most voting systems are biased towards the solutions that were submitted the earliest. Early submissions get seen more often in the beginning and therefore get more votes. As a result, they become popular early on and continue to gain popularity. Think about this in the context of YouTube. A fantastic video with one hundred views today may not be seen very often. But the video of a mouse riding a bicycle with four million views today will probably have six million views by next week. Popularity begets popularity. There are more sophisticated "randomized" voting systems that exist to avoid this problem, ensuring that every entry gets seen by the same number of voters. But these approaches are not widely used and are only effective when you have a large number of voters willing to look at a large number of submissions.
- Unless the submissions are anonymous–and they rarely are–people will naturally vote for the solutions submitted by their friends. In many organizations, people lobby for their solutions to receive votes. It becomes a popularity contest where individuals vote for the person, not the solution. This is not necessarily bad. Suppose someone has taken the time to rally the troops to support their idea. In that case, that is a good indicator of the submitter's enthusiasm, suggesting their idea might have a higher likelihood of success.
- People vote for self-serving solutions or ideas. This problem is exacerbated using a suggestion box rather than a challenge-centered approach. People will naturally vote for ideas that make *their* life better. It is human nature for self-interest to trump organizational needs.
- Most employees do not look at the big picture. Again, this is a more significant problem with idea platforms

than challenge platforms. When down in the weeds, employees sometimes fail to see what is needed and only look for solutions to things in their own peripheral vision. Unfortunately, these perspectives are not necessarily linked to customer needs or the company's overall strategic roadmap.

In general, what we find is that crowds are better at eliminating the duds than they are at picking the winners. Therefore, a potentially effective method is to use crowds to kill terrible ideas so that experts can review the remaining plausible solutions. If you can eliminate 90 percent of the "chaff" using this method, you can radically speed up your review times. Some more sophisticated methods (e.g., evaluating the standard deviation of rankings by the crowd to avoid false negatives) are more complicated and only add incremental value.

Although we often hear about the "wisdom of crowds," in reality, personal prejudices tend to bias the process. When crowdsourcing focuses on "how something should be done" (solutions) rather than "what should be done" (voting), we can tap into the true intelligence of the masses more effectively.

 *Crowdsourcing is not intended to be a democratic tool designed to gather the whims and wishes of individuals. It is intended to source solutions, not opinions.*

---

*AUTHOR'S NOTE: This tip was originally called "Crowds are Better at Eliminating Duds Than at Picking Winners." But I wanted to include mobsourcing in the title as I think that's the more important concept. In* Invisible Solutions, *I talk about another mobsourcing example: Boaty McBoatface. You can watch me tell this story to 2,000 accountants. You will definitely get a laugh out of it. https://vimeo.com/innovationguru/ boaty And if you want some scientific studies on the impact of mobsourcing, read my article, "The Ignorance of the Masses Cancels Out the Knowledgable Majority." https://stephenshapiro.com/ignorance-of-the-masses/*

# STRATEGY

## INNOVATION STRATEGY AND CUSTOMERS

Customers must be at the heart of your innovation strategy. But do you really understand their wants and needs? Most organizations do not. Go beyond focus groups, surveys, and data mining. Understand their unarticulated and subconscious pains. Once you do this, you can build an innovation strategy to differentiate your organization and dominate the competition.

# 13

## LESSONS FROM INDIANA JONES

In 1989's *Indiana Jones and the Last Crusade,* the nerdy archeology professor Indiana Jones advises students to "forget any ideas you've got about lost cities, exotic travel and digging up the world. We do not follow maps to buried treasure, and 'X' never, ever marks the spot."

Although Dr. Jones is an academic, he is really more of an adventurer. He travels the world, uncovering lost civilizations and finding buried treasures.

In today's world of data mining and customer analytics, studying your customers from the comfort of your desk can be easy. And this somewhat "academic" approach will certainly give you insights into your customers' buying habits, usability behaviors, and other consumer patterns. But most likely, you are only gathering data about *your* customers. As a result, you are missing the data of former customers and people who never were customers. As for your current customers, you will only be able to analyze their activities associated with your existing products and services; you won't be able to identify unarticulated needs.

The real treasure can be found when you leave your office, don your fedora and bullwhip, and study customers with your own two eyes.

Anthropologists and innovation experts call this ethnography, a term used to describe any research that aims to provide an in-depth description of everyday life and practices.

Instead of asking your customers questions or analyzing data, you observe them. By doing this, you can find their unarticulated wants and needs. Make sure you listen to lost customers and potential customers, as well as current customers. Information from defecting customers can flag changes in customer tastes and the competitive environment or slippage in some aspect of your organization's value proposition (e.g., quality problems). In contrast, potential customers can suggest new sources of value.

One client of mine decided to try this approach. They publish textbooks for students and instruction manuals for teachers and professors. It wasn't until they started to watch the teachers in the classroom that they developed some interesting product enhancements. For example, during one ethnographic study, the publisher found that teachers lugged several weighty books from class to class. This led the publisher to create a segmented version of the instruction manuals. This enabled teachers to carry only the section of the book they needed that week instead of an entire semester's worth of paper. It is worth noting that teachers never made this suggestion during surveys and focus groups.

These studies can also lead to exciting process improvements. A manufacturer of copying machines wanted to speed up the time it took for a technician to perform copier repairs. While observing customers using their equipment, the company discovered that most repairs were relatively simple, but customers were clueless about how to fix the problem. The solution? They supplied customers with detailed instructions on how to fix the most common jamming problems so that the customers, not technicians, could solve those problems immediately.

Whirlpool developed pedestals and storage units for its Duet front-loading washers and dryers by observing a woman who had placed her dryer upon cinderblocks to make loading and unloading easier without having to bend over. Although the pedestal's primary benefit is raising the appliances about a foot off the floor, making it easier to load and unload, the additional weight also helps anchor the machine, minimizing "washer walk." In addition, the drawers that slide out from the pedestals provide an out-of-the-way space to store laundry detergent, bleach, and fabric softener bottles.

Get out from behind your computer and see the world—and your customers—with fresh eyes. In doing this, you are sure to discover opportunities you never expected. And in the process, you might just find gold.

> **The real treasure is found when you leave your office, don your fedora and bullwhip, and study customers with your own two eyes.**

AUTHOR'S NOTE: *Sometimes, observation can lead to a new business opportunity. Two entrepreneurs separately observed the difficulties people had with taking their medication. One saw how difficult it was for his father to keep track of his medicines after having surgery. The other delivered prescriptions as a teenager and observed how difficult it was for patients to deal with multiple medications. From these observations, in 2012, PillPack was born. This online service sorts and packages patients' pills by date and time. In 2018, they were acquired by Amazon for nearly one billion dollars.*

## 14

## YOUR MARKET RESEARCH SUCKS

I magine you are a hearing aid manufacturer and want to develop the next generation of product. You conduct surveys and focus groups and discover that nearly 80 percent of the hearing-impaired population, despite their healthcare provider's recommendations, refuse to wear hearing aids, mainly citing cost as the key reason. What do you do?

The obvious answer is finding ways to produce a lower-cost hearing aid. Or is it?

Oticon, a large global manufacturer of hearing aids, wasn't convinced. It realized that its market research only gathered information at a "conscious" level: what the consumers said to it in focus groups and surveys. But the company wanted deeper insights. So it employed a number of techniques for tapping into the subconscious minds of potential customers.

It eventually discovered the real reason people did not want to wear a hearing aid: It made consumers feel flawed, stigmatized, and old, especially those individuals with early stages of hearing loss in their forties and fifties.

Although making the devices even smaller or nearly invisible might seem like the correct answer, further research found that this would only reinforce the consumers' negative feelings, as it confirmed in their minds that a hearing aid was something to be ashamed of.

Based on these new insights, Oticon took a very different route: It made large yet fashionable hearing aids that look more like earrings and are offered in bright colors and patterns, from the colors of one's alma mater to zebra stripes. During a trial study of people who wore the device for a few weeks, some users said their friends mistook their hearing aids for Bluetooth headsets. In the end, the product was a hit with consumers, and it even won several design awards.

Oticon learned that what consumers say in surveys and focus groups often contradicts what they actually think and feel and how they will ultimately act. The key is to tap into the subconscious minds of your customers because it is the subconscious mind that really drives behavior.

### Your Customers Don't Know What They Don't Know

Innovators looking for input from consumers must assume that consumers cannot always (and may not want to) explain themselves, their behaviors, their attitudes, and their decision-making processes. The average person is only aware of about 5 percent of their thoughts and feelings on any given topic. When asked outright, consumers will, of course, provide answers, but those answers may be incomplete at best and quite misleading at worst. How often have you heard representative consumers say in response to a direct question, "I will definitely buy this product," only to see the product fail (think "New Coke," the 1985 reformulation of Coca-Cola that was a colossal failure despite positive focus group feedback)? Innovators must find ways to bypass the rational, explicit, conscious mind and tap into the subconscious.

One way to do this is through the use of metaphors and storytelling. Humans think and speak in metaphors. According to

Kendall Haven, author of *Story Proof*, in the English language, five to six metaphors are used per minute in everyday speech. Just try expressing your ideas, emotions, and attitudes without using metaphors. It is almost impossible and certainly makes for a very bland conversation. Note that even the word "bland" is a metaphor in this context. Metaphors are based on human experiences and help us make sense of the world. When Oticon wanted to overcome the shortcoming of focus groups and other traditional market research techniques, it decided to use a metaphor-driven approach called The Zaltman Metaphor Elicitation Technique (ZMET®). This involves in-depth one-on-one interviews and helps consumers express their vision of how a product might fit into their lives, fill a need, or solve a problem. Lindsay Zaltman, managing director of Olson Zaltman, the consulting firm that conducted Oticon's research, found that wearing a hearing aid was like having "a neon sign on your forehead saying, 'I'm flawed, I'm old.'" Now, that's a pretty powerful metaphor.

Designworks USA, a division of BMW, uses a different approach to capture the subconscious needs of consumers. While designing cars and other products such as cell phones, computers, and tractors, instead of starting with the basic functions and features, the company has consumers tell them stories about emotion. Its designers first meet with company executives, employees, and customers to capture the emotion customers will *feel* when using this product. This is done using sketch artists rather than words. Only after everyone agrees on these emotions will the design of the form and style begin.

According to an Accenture study of executives in 639 companies, the number one reason for innovation failure was that their products and services "failed to meet customer needs." Innovators tend to build solutions around customers' explicitly articulated needs, often based on numerical data. But in doing so, the "real" consumer needs are missed. As innovators, we need to tap into the darkest recesses of the mind in order to capture what the consumer really wants.

 *The average person is only aware of about 5 percent of their thoughts and feelings on any given topic. When asked outright, consumers will provide answers, but those answers may be incomplete at best and quite misleading at worst.*

---

*AUTHOR'S NOTE: Admittedly, this tip might be one of the most complicated to implement. The best way to learn more is to dig deeper into the ZMET method. One place to start is Gerald and Lindsay Zaltman's book,* Marketing Metaphoria: What Deep Metaphors Reveal About the Minds of Consumers *(Harvard Business Review Press, 2008).*

# 15

# BE THE ASPIRIN FOR YOUR CUSTOMERS' PAINS

I magine you are scanning the cover of a men's health magazine. You see two similar headlines: "Lose Your Gut Fast" and "Get Six Pack Abs." Which of these headlines do you think is more likely to sell magazines?

Although most people intuitively think that the second headline, "Get Six Pack Abs," is the sure winner, when a website did a comparison, it found that "Lose Your Gut Fast" was read significantly more times.

Why?

## Meet People Where They Are

This phenomenon is explained nicely by the Austrian economist Ludwig von Mises, who once said that three requirements must be present for an individual to make a shift:

- The individual must be dissatisfied with the current state of affairs.
- They must see a better state.
- They must believe that they can reach that better state.

That last bullet point is critical regarding the "gut" issue. Although six-pack abs are desirable, when someone is twenty pounds overweight, it might seem like too much work to achieve the desired result. Only when your gut is gone will six-pack abs seem like a possibility. A follow-up study found that the people most interested in getting six-pack abs were those who did not have a gut to lose.

To be clear, this is not a health conversation but one related to marketing and innovation. You must "meet people where they are." That is, you need to solve their pain (e.g., a gut) before you can get them excited about any other gain (e.g., six-pack abs).

## Losses Versus Gains

This concept is further illustrated by a question I ask my audiences whenever I give a speech. Which would you prefer?

- *OPTION 1:* a guaranteed gain of $75,000?
- *OPTION 2:* an 80 percent chance of gaining $100,000 with a 20 percent chance of getting nothing?

When I ask the audience this question, 75 percent choose option 1. This percentage is consistent across all groups, regardless of audience members.

What about the following? Which would you choose?

- *Option 3:* a certain loss of $75,000?
- *Option 4:* an 80 percent chance of losing $100,000 with a 20 percent chance of not losing anything?

When audiences answer this one, 99 percent choose option 4.

Option 1 is about playing it safe when a gain is a stake. Option 4 is about taking risks when a loss is at stake.

Interestingly, when you look at these options, even though most people choose options 1 and 4, options 2 and 3 probabilistically give you better returns. On average, you will gain $80,000 with option two and will lose $80,000 with option 4.

In general, people will take greater risks to minimize (or reduce) their pain/losses, yet are risk averse when the option is to increase their pleasure/gain.

Advertising agencies know this well. For example, instead of providing peace of mind, insurance companies paint a picture of what would be lost if a catastrophic event occurred and the person was not insured.

Activists are also aware of this. According to author Barry Schwartz, "Appeals to women to do breast self-exams that emphasize the benefits of early cancer detection (gains) are less effective than those that emphasize the costs of late detection (losses)."

Instead of selling customers on how great your product or service is, show them the downside of using a less reliable alternative. When selling her high-priced service, one colleague asks, "If you needed open heart surgery, would you shop for a cardiologist based on price?" She then launches into the risk associated with not using her top-notch service.

Why is this knowledge necessary for innovation?

### Eliminate a Pain and They Will Come

We often hear the expression, "Build it and they will come." With innovation, a more accurate statement is, "Eliminate a pain and they will come." The automated teller machine (ATM) 's ultimate success is a great example.

In the mid-1970s, Citibank was the second-largest bank. In 1977, after investing hundreds of millions of dollars in ATM technology research and development, Citibank installed machines across New York City. At first, they were not very popular. The technology was confusing to first-time users, the machines were not always accurate (they sometimes dispensed the wrong amount of money), and they were impersonal. According to one person involved in the ATM rollout, customers who used ATMs were so frustrated that many closed their Citibank accounts.

The ATM may never have been a hit if it weren't for a natural disaster.

February 1978 will always be remembered for a blizzard that dumped as much as four feet of snow in the Northeast. Nearly two feet of snow in New York City brought the city to a grinding halt. Banks weren't open. Instead, people got their money by cashing checks at local supermarkets. But most of the supermarkets quickly ran out of money.

This created a massive "pain."

Where did people turn? The ATMs. It is estimated that during the storms, use of the machines increased by over 20 percent. Soon after, Citibank started running TV ads showing people trudging through the snow drifts in New York City. That's when the company introduced its wildly popular slogan, "The Citi Never Sleeps." This was the real birth of the automated teller machine.

By 1981, Citibank's market share of New York deposits had doubled, with a lot of the growth attributed to the ATM.

This story illustrates an innovator's dilemma and opportunity. The masses often do not immediately adopt brilliant innovations, and some ideas need time to incubate and gain acceptance. But will your business survive long enough to see success?

People take massive risks to eliminate their pains but play it safe when adding convenience. ATMs were primarily about convenience. What did it take for them to become a success? A pain caused by a natural disaster.

Think about the last mattress commercial you heard. They all say the same thing: "Buy our xyz bed and you will get your best night's sleep ever." Yawn. Boring. The commercial may put me to sleep, but it's not going to get me to buy a bed.

Now consider this actual radio advertisement. "If your mattress is ten years old, it weighs twice its original weight due to the dust mites that accumulate over the years." Ouch! This creates pain and makes me want to replace my mattress immediately.

Are your new ideas solving a problem? If they are just a convenience, what can you do to take advantage of pain without relying on a natural disaster?

 *We often hear the expression, "Build it and they will come." But with innovation, a more accurate statement is "Eliminate a pain and they will come."*

---

*AUTHOR'S NOTE: The topic of pain versus gain is one of great interest to me. My next book covers this topic extensively in a section on making your products and services desirable. Ludwig von Mises's perspective fascinates me as it examines the key levers companies can use to get customers interested. In particular, the third aspect–they must believe they can reach that better state–is crucial. When looking at your innovation efforts, consider how easy you can make it for customers to switch to you and then how you can make it difficult for them to leave.*

# 16

# INNOVATE WHERE YOU DIFFERENTIATE

I n his book *Animal Farm*, George Orwell writes, "All animals are equal, but some animals are more equal than others."

This is an important mantra to remember when creating an innovation program. All capabilities are equal, but some are more equal than others. You don't innovate the same way for each capability in your business. And how you innovate will not be the same as how your competitors innovate.

When I conduct executive training, one of my favorite activities requires participants to consider a typical set of capabilities common in the insurance industry: developing products and services, customer service, managing revenues, managing distribution channels, marketing products and services, underwriting, claims fulfillment, managing provider networks, and planning and managing the enterprise.

I then ask the group which capability is the most important to an insurance company. Quite often, the first answer will be claims fulfillment. "Why?" I ask, and they say, "Because this is why customers get insurance in the first place." I agree that claims fulfillment is very important, but not the *most* important.

Someone will then suggest managing revenues (or underwriting) because this is how the company makes money. Again, I commend them for their answer, but it is still not the most important capability. After nearly every process has been suggested, I stop the group and say, "Okay, I am going to give you the answer to this one: 'It depends.'"

**Different Strokes for Different Folks**

Consider four insurance companies serving relatively similar markets.

- *Unum Insurance:* Unum is the market leader in disability insurance, a firm that differentiates itself by assessing and pricing risk. Unum claims, for example, to have such finely tuned data that it can distinguish the difference in risk between left-handed and right-handed doctors who drive Volvos and live in New Jersey.
- *Progressive Insurance:* In the late 1990s, when Progressive decided to compete against the more prominent players, it chose to do so by changing how claims were processed, becoming one of the most profitable firms in the industry. Progressive's loss adjusters operated from vans with cellular communication links and computer workstations. Driving around their assigned territories, they were often at the scene of an accident before the police. In many cases, claims were processed on the spot, and it has been known for a check to be handed over by the company's loss adjusters at the site of an accident.
- *State Farm:* Competitive positioning for State Farm depends on its exclusive (and extensive) network of agents and offices. Its wide geographic coverage is reinforced by its motto: "Like a Good Neighbor, State

Farm Is There." The firm differentiates itself from the rest of the pack through this slogan and network.

- *USAA:* The customers of USAA are primarily in the transient, mobile military services, and the company is known for providing great help to this niche group. At one time, USAA was the world's largest user of toll-free numbers, which it used as the primary means to communicate with customers. All of their innovation efforts focus on improving the lives of their customers (called "members"). These investments have paid off as *Business Week* continually ranks USAA as one of the top customer service companies across all industries.

What is the most important capability to Unum? It is underwriting. For Progressive, its source of differentiation is claims fulfillment. For State Farm, its distribution network is critical because it deals with a broad swath of the population. Lastly, USAA is focused on customer service. Capabilities that are strategic for one organization may well be less critical for another in the same industry. All four of these companies are essentially in the same business, but each concentrates on a different capability to achieve a competitive advantage in the marketplace.

What is *your* most important capability? There is typically a very long and uncomfortable silence when I ask this question of CEOs, top executives, and employees. Most people do not think of their business in these terms. And as you will see in the next tip, clearly defining your focus will help you allocate your innovation investments.

Of course, this does not mean you only need to excel at one part of your business. The purpose is to help you identify your differentiators, which will often change over time. For example, Progressive Insurance is currently best known not for its Immediate Response Vehicles but rather for its ability to offer quotes from its competitors along with its own.

So, what is your most important capability? Although the question is simple, the answer requires significant reflection and alignment, and answering this question is important for determining your innovation strategy. In particular, it helps you focus your limited innovation investments on the capabilities that will yield the most significant impact.

 *All capabilities are equal, but some are more equal than others. You don't innovate the same way for each capability in your business. And how you innovate will not be the same as how your competitors innovate.*

---

*AUTHOR'S NOTE: Differentiation is a critical topic for innovation. It helps you target your investments. From my research over the past twenty-five years, I've found there are five Ds necessary to drive differentiation: Distinctive (it stands out), Desirable (customers and stakeholders want it), Durable (it stands the test of time and is difficult for others to replicate), Dynamic (it provides a solid foundation on which you can shift when necessary), and Disseminated (it is shared internally and externally). I created a short video where I discuss the 5Ds. https://vimeo.com/innovationguru/5ds. Be sure to watch it if you want to go deeper into this topic.*

**17**

## EVER NOTICE HOW "ONE SIZE FITS ALL" NEVER REALLY FITS ALL?

O nce you identify your "most important" capability, you can use this information to develop your operating strategy–how you run your business. Below is a simple framework called the Innovation Targeting Matrix (ITM) that I use to help organizations identify the right strategies for their business.

| DIFFERENTIATING | Innovate |
|---|---|
| CORE | Automate<br>Simplify<br>Outsource |
| SUPPORT | Eliminate<br>Minimize<br>Outsource |

The ITM illustrates how capabilities fall into three levels of strategic importance (from least to most strategic): "support," "core," and "differentiating."

*Support capabilities* are necessary for running the business, yet they are not your core business. Often, these are considered departments like HR, IT, or finance.

- *Operating Strategy:* Support work should be minimized and outsourced as much as possible.
- Cost containment is the primary strategy while still ensuring high quality.

*Core capabilities* are critical to your business but are not your source of competitive advantage. These create direct value for the customer. A manufacturing company's core capabilities might include order fulfillment, order acquisition, and product support. Quite often, these capabilities are "transactional" in nature.

- *Operating Strategy:* Core work should be simplified and automated whenever possible. The objective is to turn these capabilities into well-oiled machines.
- Efficiency is the primary goal.

*Differentiating capabilities* are those that set you apart from your competition. These are your most important capabilities, as described in the previous tip. Ideally, you only have one or two of these capabilities. At USAA, for example, this is Customer Service.

- *Operating Strategy:* Differentiating work is typically knowledge work and is where you want to make the most significant investment. Ideally, you want to empower knowledge workers to deliver non-cookie-cutter results that will continually set you apart from your competitors.
- Innovation is the primary strategy.

There are several important points to note with this model:

- *Make Sure Your Core is Working Before You Innovate:* Because innovation seems glamorous, companies often focus on differentiators before they have a good foundation. This is a mistake. You must have your "core" capabilities working well (efficient, low error rates, high service levels) before you can start worrying about your differentiators.

- *Use This Targeting Approach At Every Level:* This model is valuable not just at the enterprise level but also within each capability. Even seemingly support capabilities have components that help differentiate the company. For example, a major consulting firm was reevaluating its corporate training curriculum and used this model to assist in the process. It first determined which classes provided capabilities necessary to beat the competition —that is, its training "differentiators." For these, in-house custom courses were developed with the help of leading universities and thought leaders. For "core" consultant skills, the firm partnered with world-class training organizations to provide tailored versions of existing training. And for less important support skills, it used off-the-shelf training modules (outsourced training).

- *Recognize that Technology Can Be a Differentiator:* Sometimes, your differentiating capability can ensure that the work of others is repeatable and predictable. We might ordinarily think of these capabilities as support: IT, finance, or HR. For example, Wal-Mart invests heavily in the ability to connect stores, warehouses, and vendors through leading-edge technology. The employees who develop these computer systems are some of Wal-Mart's most valuable knowledge workers.

- *You Can't Catch Your Competition:* If you are number two or number three (or worse) in your industry, your differentiating capability should ideally be different than that of your leading competitors. When you are playing catch-up, changing the rules of the game is critical. It is hard to beat someone at *their* game.
- *Your Differentiators Should be Difficult to Replicate:* If your differentiating capability is easy for your competition to replicate, it probably is not a differentiator. One company that offers service warranties on water heaters and other appliances claimed its "offerings"–the bundling and pricing of its services–was its competitive differentiator. When I asked the group, "How long after introducing a new offering does your competition offer the same deal?" The answer was "in as little as two weeks." Clearly, that was not a good differentiator. After digging further, we found that their deep relationships with third-party repair technicians were distinctive and unassailable. This was a great differentiator. Unless you want to reinvent yourself every week, you should find a differentiator that is difficult to replicate and is uniquely yours.

Understanding your differentiators is important. This is a critical component of any company's business strategy. And it is equally important to know how those differentiators translate into your innovation strategy. This helps cascade priorities down to the lowest levels of the organization. It helps to focus investments on the areas of innovation that will create the most significant returns. And it enables you to determine which challenges will most likely help move the needle forward for your organization.

**It is important to know how your differentiators translate into your innovation strategy. This helps cascade priorities down to the lowest levels of the organization.**

---

*AUTHOR'S NOTE: One point I did not make clear in the original book is that functions are never support, core, or differentiating. Every person in every department performs tasks at all three levels. If the Innovation Targeting Matrix concept interests you, please read my latest book, PIVOTAL. Its sole focus is on helping you "innovate where you differentiate." I also discuss it briefly in this video, where I also explore the 5Ds of Differentiation: https://vimeo.com/innovationguru/5ds*

# 18

# BEST PRACTICES ARE (SOMETIMES) STUPID

I play golf–not well, but I play golf. My handicap is in the double digits. For me, to shoot par would be a dream. But for Tiger Woods, par would be a nightmare. I am reminded of this comparison when I see companies that are satisfied to focus on their understanding of "par," otherwise known as best practice. It was once an admirable aim but is not sufficient today. Your competitors are more like Tiger Woods than they are like me. Par won't keep you alive in the current environment. Once something becomes a best practice, it is no longer a best practice.

Innovation is about adaptability, your ability to change to stay one step ahead of the competition. When you copy someone's best practice, you are not staying ahead; you are playing a game of catch-up. Your differentiating capability, in particular, must be unique and distinctive and not based on what others are doing. When Progressive Insurance wanted to compete with the more prominent and established players, it did not use best practices; it created the Immediate Response Vehicles, something unique to the industry.

**The Best Use for Best Practices**

However, having said that I am not against best practices altogether. I am primarily against using them as your innovation strategy for your "differentiating" capabilities.

Here are a few places where best practices can be useful:

- *Internal Sharing:* If you find a practice that works well within one part of your organization, share it with others internally. Assuming your organization has shared differentiators, practices within one division or department may work well in others.
- *Core and Support:* Best practices can be helpful for core and support capabilities (see the previous tip). These capabilities should run like a well-oiled machine with high quality and low cost. But these capabilities will not help you stand out in a crowded marketplace. Even then, I consider these "proven" practices not necessarily the best ones.
- *Practices from Outside Your Industry:* You can get incredible innovations from companies that are not your competition. In fact, I encourage you to "steal with pride" from companies outside your industry. For example, South West Airlines did this when it benchmarked an Indianapolis 500 pit crew to improve plane turn-around time. Hospitals have gained new insights by studying the check-in process of hotels. And a mail-order office supply company improved the return of empty toner cartridges by applying Netflix's DVD subscription process. Sometimes these cross-industry practices can lead to revolutionary innovations.
- *Your Innovation Process:* Although you want to focus your innovation efforts on *your* differentiating capabilities, unless you are an innovation company (like IDEO), *how*

you innovate is probably not a differentiator. For example, if you are an insurance company, you want to apply innovation to your claims processing if claims processing is a differentiator. But the innovation process is only a core capability. There is no point in your inventing new innovation methods. Therefore you should use innovation best practices wherever and whenever possible. Reading this book will give you a number of those practices.

Best practices are not an innovation strategy. Copying the competition will only help you achieve parity. Only when you fully understand your innovation targeting strategy can you determine where best practices are helpful and where they are a waste of time.

 *Your competitors are like Tiger Woods. Par (aka best practice) won't keep you alive in the current environment.*

---

*AUTHOR'S NOTE: This chapter was the inspiration for the title of this book. If you skipped it, please read the preface, where I describe the three reasons best practices are stupid. This tip also shows how successful companies don't rest on their laurels. When this book was originally written, Netflix was only a DVD-by-mail subscription service. But as internet bandwidth improved, they became a video streaming service. Then, to increase their competitive position, they created their own programming, starting with* House of Cards. *Lately, they have focused on creating different subscription models, including an advertising subsidized model. They also recently shut down their DVD subscription service. The need to innovate never ends.*

## 19

---

# SIMPLIFICATION IS THE BEST INNOVATION

T he author of *The Little Prince*, Antoine de Saint-Exupery, once said, "Perfection is finally attained not when there is no longer anything to add but when there is no longer anything to take away."

Unfortunately, most innovators believe perfection involves adding as many features and functions as possible. As a result, new products are often overly complex and end up "overserving" their customers.

Microsoft Office is a perfect example of this. While 99 percent of the software's functionality goes unused, these complexities can negatively impact the experience for novice users. Being able to do everything for everyone is not perfection.

### Make Your Products More Accessible

Instead, focus on making your products "more accessible." Accessible can have a variety of meanings.

The video game market has always been enamored with increasingly faster machines and higher-quality graphics. But the Nintendo Wii changed that. Instead of creating more sophisticated and complicated games that would appeal to the advanced gamer, they created an interface that would appeal to people ages eight and eighty alike. That's accessibility. In 2008, 10.2 million Wii units were sold in the United States, compared to only 4.7 million Xbox 360s and 3.5 million PlayStation 3s. And a significant amount of money was being made on all of the Wii add-ons. Since then, competitors like Xbox 360's Kinect have been fast to replicate the Wii's success, creating a whole new level of competition.

Service-based organizations can make their offerings more affordable and accessible by turning them into physical or digital products that require little or no human intervention.

- Cybersettle automates insurance claims processing.
- My Personality Poker® cards enable people to re-create one of my most popular presentations at a fraction of the cost.
- Self-assessment tools can reduce reliance on consultants.
- Remote diagnostic technologies can speed up medical exams and pre-qualify patients before they visit the doctor.
- PlumChoice enables technicians to fix computers through remote access, saving customers money and eliminating the need to bring the machine to the repair store. In 2018, The Allstate Corporation acquired the business and merged it into their SquareTrade division.
- Legalzoom.com offers affordable legal advice for people who might otherwise not seek counsel.
- TurboTax simplifies tax filing.
- Ernst & Young Consulting once offered a subscription service, Ernie, which provided small businesses with a low-cost online alternative to high-priced consulting. When Capgemini acquired the consulting firm, Ernie was shut down.

- Experts convert their intellectual property into books, MP3s, DVDs, digitally delivered training (including e-learning) systems or online databases.

And the possibilities are endless.

Another option is to develop a low-cost version of your products and services. Examine why people are really using your products/services and the bare minimum ways of delivering the desired outcome. Three-hundred-dollar netbooks (which evolved into Google's Chromebooks) are popular because they are stripped-down computers, and most people just want to do word processing and surf the internet. Apple's iPad takes this one step further by making an intuitive user interface in an incredibly light product, making it accessible to technophiles and technophobes alike. And for the first time, smartphones are now outselling computers.

Dow Corning, the maker of silicone-based products, has traditionally been in the low-volume, high-service business. To make their product more accessible and affordable, they launched a high-volume, low-service business. This business sells purely through the internet with no call centers, and the product can only be ordered in bulk. Although this model cannibalized some of Dow Corning's core business, on the whole, it grew the entire business considerably, giving them access to buyers who would never have used them previously.

Which features, services, or qualities can be reduced to tap into a new market?

Michelangelo once said, "In every block of marble, I see a statue as plain as though it stood before me, shaped and perfect in attitude and action. I have only to hew away the rough walls that imprison the lovely apparition to reveal it to the other eyes as mine see it." My guess is a lot of useless features, functions, and expensive services are covering up your masterpiece.

> *"Perfection is finally attained not when there is no longer anything to add but when there is no longer anything to take away."—Antoine de Saint- Exupéry.*

---

*AUTHOR'S NOTE: When working with my clients, one of the first questions we explore is, "What do we need to kill?" Knowing what to stop doing is as important as knowing what to do. This frees time so you can invest in other, more meaningful endeavors. Unfortunately, we tend to fall in love with our projects and ideas. One reason for this is something called confirmation bias. In tip 25, we explore the role of confirmation bias as a destroyer of innovation.*

# MEASURES

## INNOVATION MEASURES AND MOTIVATION

All executives know that measurements are essential to running any business. But do your measures stimulate ingenuity and foster efficient innovation? Or are they inadvertently killing creativity and encouraging less-than-desirable behaviors? Successful innovation requires understanding psychology, neuroscience, motivational theory, and the scientific method. Armed with this information, you can motivate people to participate in innovation and minimize the risks associated with failure.

# 20

# MOTIVATE LIKE MASLOW

S keeball is an arcade game where players "bowl" for points. During my childhood, it was hugely popular. Why? What motivated kids to part with their hard-earned allowance money to play this game? Of course, it was fun. But more important, it was one of the first arcade games to give you tickets based on the points you got. These could be redeemed for silly prizes like candy, fake vampire fangs, or rubber spiders. Although the most desirable prizes required thousands of tickets and were out of the reach of nearly every player, we played anyway, cherishing each ticket we won.

The motivation technique that got us as children to part with our quarters is still used in corporations today to get people to participate in innovation efforts. Let's explore a few of the most popular methods.

## Extrinsic Motivators

Although cash bonuses for new innovations have been around for ages, more sophisticated methods have gained popularity recently. One involves the use of a points system. When you contribute an idea, solution, comment or vote, you get points–much like American Express Membership Rewards points or skeeball tickets–that can be used to buy various items: company T-shirts, mugs, and other "exciting" goodies.

Some companies have taken the concept a bit further and allow people to accumulate points that can be used in auctions. Once a month, the company holds an auction for a trip to, say, Tahiti. Anyone with points can join the bidding. This encourages people to earn and save as many points as possible to have a chance at some huge prizes.

Another model that doesn't necessarily need a points system involves "priceless" awards. Remember the MasterCard commercials? Dinner with the CEO, a prime parking space, or an extra week of vacation; these types of prizes are great motivators because no amount of money can buy them.

All of these models have an extrinsic form of motivation in common. They all offer a tangible prize. Chip Conley, author of *Peak*, would point out that these motivators relate to the lowest rungs on Abraham Maslow's hierarchy of needs–five levels of human needs where higher-level needs are not felt until lower-level needs have been satisfied. The lowest two levels involve physiology (e.g., food and shelter) and safety/ security. Extrinsic motivations, such as money, allow you to meet these basic human needs.

Yet there is an opportunity for other, potentially more effective forms of motivation for innovation.

## The Work is Its Own Reward

At the highest level of Maslow's hierarchy, you find "self-actualization." In the innovation/business world, this is where "the work is its own reward." The open-source software movement was primarily built on this model. Millions of people helped develop software without any formal extrinsic compensation. Many do it just because it "feels good to contribute." For some, it is about building software to bring down the "evil empire"–whichever company that might be.

While working in Formula 1–ultrafast car racing–I learned the power of this highest level of motivation. At the manufacturing plant where the cars are produced, the job is similar to that of workers at traditional automotive manufacturers. But the race team employees work longer hours, often for less pay than their traditional counterparts. Why? They love their job. It's not *what* they are doing that matters. It is *why* they are doing it that is their motivation. Being part of a winning racing team spurs them to perform at their best.

Although this "work is its own reward" is an incredibly effective motivator in some situations, as illustrated above, it is challenging to implement in a "typical" organization.

## Status and Recognition

A third type of motivation lies between safety/physiology and self-actualization and relates to Maslow's love/belonging and self-esteem: status and recognition. This can be highly effective, especially in organizations where people are hired mainly for their degrees and intelligence.

For some individuals, being recognized by their peers, in particular, is the highest form of motivation. In some circles, being published in a peer-reviewed journal is among the highest honors to be bestowed on someone.

Therefore, find ways of recognizing people, especially when it involves peer recognition. The name of the game is status.

If you use a points system like the ones described above, one way to do this is to create a leaderboard. This creates friendly competition in the workplace and helps individuals stand out from the crowd based on their contributions.

Another approach is to develop a good recognition program as part of your communication plans. Many companies do this, but they rarely do it well.

Here's the real opportunity...

## Stop Recognizing People for Doing Their Jobs

Stop recognizing people for doing their jobs. When you hire someone to work for you, they should be expected to have a basic level of competence. Recognizing people for doing what they are hired to do reinforces a culture where the status quo is good enough.

Instead, recognize and reward people for going beyond their jobs and for doing unexpected things.

If you want to encourage open innovation or cross-business unit collaboration, recognize people for that. If you want employees to take risks, make a big deal out of individuals who do so. If you want to let people know that failure is acceptable–when done correctly–then highlight situations where something didn't work as planned, yet powerful lessons were learned.

When you shift the conversations throughout your organization, you change the culture. These motivation programs are an excellent opportunity to create an environment of innovation and promote the values important to your organization.

There is no one-size-fits-all approach to motivating employees. Each individual has different needs and wants. But when done correctly, a good recognition-and-rewards program can make the skeeball model of motivation seem like child's play.

 **Stop recognizing people for doing their jobs. When you hire someone to work for you, it should be expected that they are competent. Recognizing people for doing what they are hired to do reinforces a culture where the status quo is good enough.**

---

*AUTHOR'S NOTE: After the book's release, I was on ABC News discussing five of the tips. The one that caught the interviewer's attention was this one. In particular, the idea that you don't want to recognize someone for doing the work they are expected to do. You can watch this five-minute interview here: https://vimeo.com/innovationguru/abcnews*

# 21

## YOU GET WHAT YOU MEASURE, BUT WILL YOU GET WHAT YOU WANT?

I n business, an old adage is, "You get what you measure." But the big question is, will you get what you want? Too many innovation-measurement systems are designed in a way that inadvertently creates undesirable behaviors. They measure the wrong things resulting in poor results.

In general, there are four types of innovation measures:

1. *Activity/Capability Measures*–These measure the activity associated with participation in your challenges and the overall innovation program (e.g., number of registered solvers, number of submissions per challenge, percentage of time invested in innovation, percentage of employees trained in innovation).

2. *Solve-Rate Measures*–These subjectively measure how well you solved your challenges (e.g., percentage of challenges that were partially solved, percentage of challenges that were solved entirely, potential value of solutions).

3. *Implementation Measures*–Finding solutions to your challenges is not enough. You need to implement the

solutions cost-effectively and timely (e.g., percentage of solutions implemented, time-to-market, implementation costs, percentage of on-time product launches).

4. *Value Realization Measures*–These measure the actual value accrued (e.g., increase in revenues, reduction in costs, percentage of revenue from innovations introduced in the last six months, overall ROI).

Of course, we want our innovation efforts to result in value–the last measure–as this is where the rubber meets the road. But sometimes, value realization can take years, or in the case of pharmaceutical companies, decades. Therefore, you need the first three measures to monitor your program's progress in the short term. These are leading indicators that can help predict long-term success.

The first category–activity and capability–are useful in measuring trends over time for things like community engagement, the effectiveness of internal communications, and the quality of challenges. But sometimes measuring activity can be misleading.

When working with clients, one of the most common activity measures is the number of solutions submitted for a given challenge. But this often leads to misleading results. Which is better: getting one hundred solutions or getting only two solutions? Although most people intuitively think one hundred is better than two, this is not necessarily true. As pointed out earlier, it is not the absolute number that matters but rather a relative number of good solutions to bad solutions. If you received one hundred solutions where only two were precisely what you needed and the other ninety-eight were duds, this is worse than getting just two that were right on the money.

Although a lot of activity is good, too many submissions can indicate that you have a poorly defined challenge. Remember that a well-defined challenge is self-vetting, preventing too many poor submissions from making it into the system. The solar activity challenge run by NASA yielded only four solutions, but one of those solutions was spot on. Therefore the ratio of good solutions to duds (aka the signal-to-noise ratio) might be a more interesting measure.

The key is to make sure you understand the unintended consequences of your measurement system, especially regarding activity measures. If used properly, these measures can help you drive higher solve rates (measure number two).

**Diagnosing Performance**

But higher solve rates do not always lead to greater value (measure number four). High solve rates with low value can indicate problems with your innovation program:

- *Poor implementation*–You are unable to convert solutions into finished products/services.
- *Poor commercialization*–Your solutions do not meet the needs of the market/customers and therefore do not generate revenue.
- *Poor relevance*–Your challenges, although solved, are not significant enough to "move the needle" of the organization's innovation efforts.

Measures are important for helping track your innovation efforts and can help diagnose potential issues, but it is essential to measure the right things. Simply shifting what you measure can significantly impact the results.

Consider the typical product development process. Research & development (R&D) people are the only ones held accountable, often developing solutions from their ivory towers. Their solutions may or may not meet customer needs and often do not meet internal business needs. One of Europe's leading medical manufacturers, in an effort to fix this problem, shifted to cross-functional teams with joint responsibility for the end result. Now, product development no longer ends at product definition. It continues until three months after product launch. Therefore, sales, marketing, manufacturing, legal, vendor management, and others are involved in this cross-functional effort. As a result, nearly 70 percent of the company's new products launched on time, compared with just 15 percent previously.

Peter Drucker once said, "If you can't measure it, you can't manage it." Yes, measures play an important role in innovation. They give a snapshot of performance, they provide early detection of potential issues, and they drive behaviors. The key is to use the right measures in a way that helps, rather than hinders innovation.

 *Too many innovation measurement systems are designed in a way that inadvertently creates undesirable behaviors.*

---

AUTHOR'S NOTE: *Measures should give us a sense of progress. But sometimes, even when we hit the numbers, we feel as though we aren't advancing enough. This might be due to "prevalence-induced concept change," a term coined by Harvard researcher Daniel Gilbert. He argues that as we diminish a problem's prevalence, we adjust our definition of that problem. So, initially, we only recognize, for example, severe safety issues or large errors. However, as we solve these, our definitions expand to include smaller issues, which can feel like a magnification of the problems. This doesn't mean progress isn't being made; it's just an emotional perspective that contradicts the rational measures. While it's beneficial to solve all problems, there can be diminishing returns. Time, money, and resources are limited. If we continue pursuing largely solved or minor issues, we might neglect more crucial business aspects. This is why measuring at the right level of detail is critical. Focus on what's important, not on what's apparent.*

# 22

# THE PERFORMANCE PARADOX

I f you want to go faster, stop focusing on speed. If you want to be more creative, stop measuring creativity. Paradoxically, when organizations hyperfocus on their goals, they are less likely to achieve them.

Let's think back to the Formula 1 racing team example for a moment. Although the cars are technological marvels, the pit crews always amazed me the most. When I worked with them, a pit crew consisted of twenty men who serviced the race cars, refueling, changing tires, and performing required maintenance in seconds. To ensure that each pit crew member was in the proper role, they would continually shift positions during practice until they found the optimal configuration of the team. A stopwatch measured their time in milliseconds. As they practiced, there came a point where no matter how hard they tried, they couldn't go any faster. Not even one one-thousandth of a second faster. This was their performance plateau, their best possible time.

Then, as an experiment, the pit crew boss told the team to concentrate *not* on their time but rather on their style. They were asked to think of the word "smooth" while changing the tires. This time, their movements were more significant than their speed.

Astonishingly, when they weren't focusing on speed, the crew shaved several tenths of a second off their best time, even though they "felt" they were going slower.

I call this the performance paradox. It occurs when overly focusing on a future goal (e.g., beating the stopwatch) may be the very thing that prevents you (and your team) from hitting your targets.

Although the general concept of counterintuitive motivation has gained pop culture status recently due to books like *Drive* by Dan Pink, the research in this area goes back to the turn of the century.

In the early 1900s, Robert Yerkes and J. D. Dodson developed the aptly named Yerkes-Dodson Law. The premise is that performance increases relative to motivation (they called it "arousal") only to a point, after which performance drops. Then, as you become "overmotivated," performance paradoxically decreases. Typically, this progression is drawn as an inverted U-shaped curve.

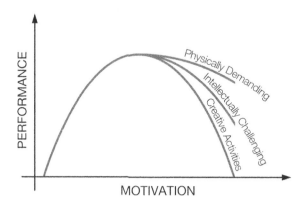

The key is to find the sweet point of optimal performance. And this usually involves a focus on the activity, not the target or goal.

Yerkes and Dodson suggested that different tasks require different arousal levels (to use their word). For example, physically demanding tasks often require higher levels of motivation. This explains why professional athletes are inclined to be more goal driven. Even so, as demonstrated by the pit crew example, too much goal orientation will hurt even athletic performance.

Within the business world, Yerkes and Dodson found that intellectually challenging tasks required lower levels of arousal/motivation to improve concentration. And the more creative the activity, the less motivation was needed to hit peak performance levels.

In fact, studies reveal that creativity often diminishes when individuals are rewarded (externally/extrinsically motivated) for doing their work. Why? The desire to achieve the goal overtakes the personal interest in the endeavor.

If a reward–money, awards, or even praise–becomes the reason for engaging in an activity, the endeavor will ultimately be viewed as less enjoyable in its own right, and the focus will shift to getting the task done quickly with minimal risk. This overshadows the intellectual stimulation of the process and kills creativity. Creativity is a process that cannot be forced.

Dr. Teresa Amabile from Harvard University once wrote that "rewards undermine creativity when [individuals feel that their] self-determination is undermined." However, "rewards can enhance creativity when they confirm competence, provide useful information in a supportive way, or enable people to do something that they were already intrinsically motivated to do."

This is often best accomplished through measures that make people feel as though they are in control rather than being controlled. Freedom to be creative (rather than mandates to be creative) enhance performance.

What can an organization do to address this performance paradox?

Just as the pit crew needed to stop focusing on the stopwatch to go faster, you and your team must stop focusing on your goals to enhance creativity and performance. This involves "being present"—a concept often difficult to embrace.

A high school student I once met had become increasingly

anxious about passing her upcoming final exam in math, which was always her weakest subject. She studied incredibly hard, but despite her efforts, she failed. The stress of performing over-stimulated her, making it difficult to concentrate. In business, we inadvertently do the same when we set tight deadlines and overly aggressive targets.

Fortunately for this student, her teachers gave her another chance. But this time, instead of concentrating on passing (the result), when she woke up each morning, she would visualize herself as Condoleezza Rice, the former U.S. secretary of state and a very successful, highly educated woman. In her mind, Dr. Rice wouldn't worry about a high school math exam, so neither should she. By imagining she was someone else, she stopped agonizing and gained more confidence. By changing her mindset and not focusing on the result, she reduced her stress and scored 93 percent, her greatest performance to date.

Why does this performance paradox take place? One reason has to do with the wiring of the brain.

The cerebellum is the place where we store practiced skills for automatic recall. Unfortunately, we become less proficient at those practiced skills when we engage the cerebral cortex–the thinking part of the brain. Overthinking kills automatic recall.

For example, say you are an excellent golfer and have practiced your swing hundreds of times. To access those skills, you need to stop thinking about them. When you are in a tournament (a stressful situation), if you try to access those practiced responses by thinking about them, you choke. These stored responses can only be accessed through relaxation. Practiced behaviors enacted in a calm environment can be used with a good deal of proficiency.

The same is true for creativity.

Most individuals are naturally creative, but we often overthink and lose our ability to do what is an innate ability. In essence, we are "choking" our ability to be creative when we think too much, feel too much stress, or are motivated extrinsically.

To increase creativity, first, be aware of the impact that stress is having on your organization's creativity. To reduce stress, encourage employees to focus on the process rather than the outcome. Add subjective measures to your performance-management system and measure people's qualitative contribution to the business, not just the quantitative numbers.

One company I know has its employees to meditate outside before embarking on any creative endeavor. Although this might exceed what most companies are comfortable doing, it reduces stress, enhances creativity, and increases overall performance.

John Cleese, best known for his role in the British comedy Monty Python, once said, "High creativity is responding to situations without critical thought...If you want creative workers, give them enough time to play."

 *If you want to go faster, stop focusing on speed. If you want to be more creative, stop measuring creativity. Paradoxically, when organizations hyperfocus on their goals, they are less likely to achieve them.*

AUTHOR'S NOTE: *The Performance Paradox is one of the lenses in* Invisible Solutions. *In that book, I say that paradoxically, the more you focus on solutions, the less likely you are to find the best solutions. Instead of answers, you want to look for better questions. Don't always focus on the goal. This concept applies to all areas of business and life. A women's clothing store ran a competition to see who could sell the most over a two-month period. Most employees chased the prize. One sales rep, however, prioritized customer service over sales, even if it meant sending customers to competitors. Surprisingly, by focusing on serving rather than selling, she outsold her peers significantly. My clients have achieved similar results when they stopped giving sales reps targets and got them to focus on value.*

# 23

# TIME PRESSURE KILLS CREATIVITY

A good friend and colleague, Scott Halford, is an authority on neurobehavior. He uses a simple yet effective exercise demonstrating time pressure's impact on creativity.

Although this demonstrates how time pressure kills creativity, it is not presented to the audience as such. Pitching it as a test of what the brain can hear and process is essential. Here's what you tell the group:

 "We will conduct an experiment to test how fast your brain works. I will read you a long list of numbers. I want you to write down as many numbers as you can. I will be speaking quite fast, so try to keep up. The person who writes down the most *correct* numbers will be the winner and will get a prize. Interspersed with the numbers will be a command to write something else down. To be eligible for the prize, you must write something, anything, for these. One last thing, you don't have the option *not* to compete. Everyone must go for the prize. Ready?"

At this point, pull out a sheet of paper. You can write down numbers in advance if you want. But it is just as easy to make up numbers while pretending to read from a blank sheet. Then, rapidly, shout out about twenty numbers—56, 789, 43, 2105, 456, 84, etc. Then, without pausing, say, "Write down a color," and immediately continue with another list of ten numbers. Then, again without pausing, say, "Write down a piece of furniture," and continue with another list of ten or so numbers. Then, without pausing, say, "Write down the name of a genius." Close with a few more numbers and tell people to put down their pens.

Now it is time to see the results. We won't focus on the numbers but only on the other commands.

Ask everyone to stand. If they did not write down a color, have them sit down. Most people should be standing. Then say, "If you wrote down blue, red, green, or yellow as the color, please sit down." Most people will sit. Ask people to list the other colors they wrote down. More than 90 percent of audiences write down these four "primary" colors because these are the colors we learned since childhood.

Next, ask everyone to stand. If someone did not write down a piece of furniture, have them sit down. Then say, "If you wrote down couch, sofa, chair, table, or desk, please sit." Most people will sit at this point. Again, these are the most common pieces of furniture.

Finally, ask everyone to stand one last time. If someone did not write down a genius, have them sit down. Then say, "If you wrote down Einstein, please sit." At this point, nearly everyone will be seated.

Here's the point: Creativity is completely eliminated when pressed for time, in this case, severely pressed for time. Novelty goes out the window. People focus on getting the job done. The fact that this exercise is set up like a competition simulates what is done in many organizations. Extrinsic motivation (the prize and bragging rights) overshadows creativity. Of course, you didn't ask people to be creative. But even if you did, it would have been challenging under these circumstances.

As a follow-up, ask people to consider a color that no one else will write down. Only give them a few seconds. Now, if you go one by one through the room, you will find a wide divergence of colors, typically two to ten times more than when under pressure (depending on the group size). Asking people to be creative and giving them a little breathing room can enhance creativity.

This is an excellent example of how time pressure or extreme stress can kill creativity. In these situations, individuals choose automatic responses that have been programmed into their brains over the years.

> **Asking people to be creative and giving them a little breathing room can enhance creativity.**

*AUTHOR'S NOTE: This is a fun activity that can be used to make a wide range of points. When I do a variation of this activity, I instead use it to show how predictable we are as human beings and why we tend to tap into past experiences when developing new solutions. It links back to tip 5–Expertise is the Enemy of Innovation. As a side note, a fun thing to do with the "genius" portion is to ask, "Who wrote down their own name or the word me?" There is almost always someone in the audience who did this, and it will get a big laugh.*

## 24

## STOP GLORIFYING FAILURE

A clothing manufacturer wanted to venture into the direct-to-consumer retail business. Rather than developing a detailed strategy based on years of analysis, it rented an empty space in a local mall and set up a trial shop in a matter of weeks. The store was set up with video cameras and other equipment to help analyze the results. Although the store concept ultimately "failed," the company learned more during two months of running the experiment than it would have spending a year analyzing the marketplace. It quickly reworked the store and tested out a second version, then continued the process with frequent iterations. Over time it increased the size of the experiments until the stores were rolled out on a national level.

Adam Savage, a co-host on the television show *MythBusters*, is known to say, "Failure is *always* an option. It is the cornerstone of our approach to the scientific method. Any result is a result."

This is a profound way to look at innovation.

When you look at and measure life–and innovation–as a series of experiments, failure takes on a whole new meaning.

## Redefine Failure

One definition of an experiment is "a test or investigation, especially one planned to provide evidence for or against a hypothesis."

An experiment can only fail if you don't gather the proper evidence. Even if the evidence proves your hypothesis was wrong, the experiment can be considered a huge success, as it will save you a lot of money in the long run. When you view innovation through the lens of experimentation, it redefines failure. Tip 9 ("What Did Edison Get Wrong About Innovation?") might appear to denigrate the value of experimentation. The reality is *someone* must experiment and "fail." And open innovation is not always appropriate or applicable.

Therefore, when developing new concepts, one approach (especially when "market" uncertainty is involved) is to create small experiments that can be scaled and measured over time. Here are four likely outcomes of an experiment:

1. The experiment validated our hypothesis. Let's make a more significant investment in a larger experiment.
2. Our original hypothesis was wrong, but we found a promising direction. Let's create a new experiment with a new hypothesis.
3. Our original hypothesis was wrong and we should kill the idea.
4. Our experiment did not give us accurate data for determining whether or not the hypothesis was correct. As a result, we might believe that the hypothesis was validated when in fact, it wasn't (or vice versa).

Of these four outcomes, only the last one is a failure. With the other three, the experiment was successful. It becomes a way to measure if we are on the right path, and it stops us from making further investments in the wrong direction.

## Build It, Try It, Fix It

One of the biggest barriers to innovation success is analysis paralysis. It is the belief that studying the marketplace ad infinitum will yield better results. This is just not true. We can never predict what will happen in the "real" world, no matter how much data we have, how many focus groups we conduct, or how many strategy consulting firms we hire.

Therefore, instead of using an "analyze, design, build, test, deploy" model, use the "build it, try it, fix it" model–build something, try it out for a while, and learn from your experiments. Each iteration gives you valuable information about the real world, not the spreadsheet world.

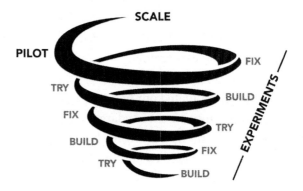

It is a simple process, and it is one used by a clothing manufacturer that wanted to venture into the retail market. Develop a small experiment where the risk of failure is limited or controllable (build it). Learn from the results (try it). Adjust the experiment (fix it). Continue to iterate with larger experiments, increasing the scale. Change directions when necessary. Stop pursuing an idea when the experiment suggests a lack of viability or desirability.

Experiments done well will focus your energies on market-ready opportunities while avoiding unnecessary investments in potential duds.

However, sometimes even well-defined experiments can give you false positives. That is, the experiment tells you a new product, service, or market is a good idea, yet in the end it proves to be a total flop. In those situations, you have a good ol'-fashioned failure on your hand.

Of course, there are productive ways to shine a light on failure. In their quest for big successes, a giant retailer had some colossal failures. Instead of chastising the people involved with the failed venture, they celebrated. It held a massive funeral. There was even a coffin where the project (not the project team) was buried.

Several years back, Intuit decided to target a younger population by linking tax filing with hip-hop. It made significant marketing investments and partnered with companies like Expedia and Best Buy. But in the end, its marketing effort proved unsuccessful, and the program was killed. How did the company handle the failure? According to *BusinessWeek*, "The team that developed the campaign documented its insights, such as the fact that Gen Yers don't visit destination websites that feel too much like advertising." Then, on a stage, in front of some 200 Intuit marketers, the team received an award from Intuit Chairman Scott Cook, who said, "It's only a failure if we fail to get the learning."

You want to be careful not to glorify failure too much. Successes can give you useful input at a much lower price tag. But if you do fail, deal with the problem head-on and learn from the experience.

One company that lives and breathes this philosophy is Koch Industries, the second largest privately held company in the United States, with approximately one hundred billion dollars in annual revenues. Charles Koch, the company's chairman, and CEO, encourages employees to build small experiments that prove or disprove hypotheses through a process the company calls "experimental discovery." In Koch's words, "Given that the market economy is an experimental discovery process, business failures are inevitable, and any attempt to eliminate them only ensures overall failure. The key is to recognize when we are experimenting and limit the bet accordingly... Encouraging experimental discovery and not penalizing well-planned experiments that fail fuels an engine of small frequent bets that generates powerful discovery and learning. This is vital to innovation, growth, and long-term profitability."

Create experiments that mitigate risk and provide insights into concept viability. Learn from these experiences while avoiding overanalysis. As an innovation colleague, Ville Keränen, once told me, "One idiot who walks gets further than five intellectuals who only talk."

 *"Failure is always an option. It is the cornerstone of our approach to the scientific method. Any result is a result."*
—*Adam Savage, cohost of television's MythBusters.*

AUTHOR'S NOTE: *When this book was first published, this tip's title was "Failure is Always an Option." But I find that the over-glorification of failure sends the wrong message. We should not strive for failure. Yes, it is an inevitable outcome of trying something new, but it should not be the goal. As mentioned above, we never want option number four (our experiment gave us the wrong data), which is truly a failure in the process. Disproving a hypothesis (number three) is highly desirable and is not a failure. Therefore, it is important to distinguish between a "busted myth" (a disproven hypothesis) and a real failure. Failure is not always an option. The next tip explains one of the biggest causes of innovation failure.*

# 25

# STOP LOVING YOUR IDEAS

B e honest. There is something about yourself that you would like to change. Maybe you think you are unattractive, over-weight, unintelligent, or unlucky. Regardless of what it is, viewing the world through that lens is how the world will be for you. It doesn't matter what evidence you receive to the contrary because you will still skillfully refute it. If you think you are unattractive and someone pays you a compliment, you will assume they want some-thing, feel bad for you, or that something must be wrong with them. We only look for and listen to the evidence that supports our beliefs. Psychologists call this "confirmation bias."

The same holds true for innovation. When you view the world through the lens that your new idea is good, you only see the evidence that supports your conclusion while subconsciously ignoring all of the points that don't. In the process, you might be making some bad innovation investments.

### Confirmation Bias

Confirmation bias is one reason individuals representing both "sides" of an argument (including politics) honestly feel they have the better argument. It is natural to focus on the strengths of our side and the weaknesses of the other side.

This concept is important to the innovation process and how you measure your innovation strategies, capabilities, and successes and failures.

Whenever you have an idea, it is human nature to search for all of the data supporting your belief. You want to prove your concept right and continue to build the case supporting your belief. But in the process, you may ignore all the signs that disprove your theory. This can have negative consequences for the organization. Once you believe your idea is good, it will be difficult for anyone to prove you wrong.

Scott Cook, CEO of Intuit, once wisely said, "For every one of our failures, we had spreadsheets that looked awesome."

For most of your failures, you probably had a lot of evidence for why it was a great idea. However, there was perhaps also a lot of evidence that did not support your idea, but you never looked for it.

Make sure that as you develop new concepts and measure their effectiveness, you look for disproving data. Find all of the evidence that refutes your beliefs and hypothesis. This is the first step towards eliminating confirmation bias.

Researchers Martin A. Tolcott and F. Freeman Marvin gave trained U.S. Army intelligence analysts a battlefield scenario. The analysts were then asked to determine the enemy's most likely avenue of approach and their confidence level with this analysis. Later, they were given three updated intelligence reports, each containing some items that supported their hypotheses and others that disproved them. They were then asked to rate each information item in terms of the degree to which it supported or contradicted their hypothesis.

What the researchers found was that analysts held on to their initial hypotheses. Even though there was significant evidence that disproved their beliefs, the new information somehow increased their confidence levels.

Tolcott and Marvin reran the test with the same participants. But before doing so, they showed participants how confirmation bias impacted their decision-making the first time. During the second trial, participants were given visual reminders designed to help foster their awareness of alternative hypotheses. The result? Generally, there was a "lower level of confidence, greater consideration of alternative enemy courses of action, and more willingness to reverse early decisions based on new evidence." In fact, during the second trial, 50 percent of the participating teams changed their hypothesis at least once during the exercise.

It is human nature to believe what we want to believe. When we get an idea, we subconsciously focus on proving those beliefs right. But being right can be the enemy of good innovation. As an innovator, don't get too attached to your ideas. Proactively play devil's advocate and look for disproving data to help you measure your innovations against the alternatives and give that data equal or greater weight. This will allow you to make better decisions on which innovations to pursue and which ones to kill.

 **As an innovator, don't get too attached to your ideas. Being right can be the enemy of good innovation.**

---

*AUTHOR'S NOTE: This tip was originally titled "View the World Through a Different Lens." But I felt that was a bit obscure, so I changed it for this edition. The main point is that we need to be a bit more skeptical about our ideas. If we love our innovations, we may subconsciously focus on evidence that supports why our ideas are great rather than seeing reality. This is a critical concept that often does not get enough airplay. As you will see in tip 35, there has been a slant towards killing the words, "Yeah, but." However, if we don't have the right checks and balances, we can move forward with innovations that should not see the light of day.*

*Loving your ideas creates confirmation bias. It also leads to another fatal error: positive test strategy. This happens when you run experiments designed only to prove that your ideas are good, forgetting to conduct experiments designed specifically to show that they might, in fact, be stinkers. When you combine these two together—i.e., confirmation bias and positive test strategy—you end up with a recipe for disaster. You could continue investing in ideas that should be killed.*

*But being aware of confirmation bias is not enough to eliminate it. For extra protection, make sure that the individuals testing the idea are not the same as those who developed it in the first place. In addition, I find it helpful to have a devil's advocate team. Their job is to uncover all the reasons that investment in an innovation should be stopped. They neutralize the positive test strategy issue by conducting experiments specifically designed to disprove the hypothesis.*

# PEOPLE

## ORGANIZATION, LEADERSHIP, AND CULTURE

Is your organization a cult? In other words, is your culture so strong that it encourages everyone to think the same way? Maybe it's time to hire people who don't "fit the mold." In fact, it may even be time for you to turn your organization upside down. Give up central control and embed innovation in every crevice. Innovation is for the people and by the people. When you treat your employees as owners of the business, you will find that they take the initiative to innovate.

# 26

---

# HIRE PEOPLE YOU DON'T LIKE

I remember a project I worked on many years ago. I was leading a large team and had a very generous budget. I chose John to co-lead with me because we got along so well. I consider myself to be creative, spontaneous, and enthusiastic, and John was pretty much the same. The team loved working with us. We were fun, engaging, and motivating.

The project was a colossal failure and massive waste of money.

The problem was that John and I got caught up in the novelty of our work. We were too focused on developing new ideas and ensuring people were happy. We never got any real work done.

In hindsight, this failure probably could have been predicted. Our working styles were just too similar.

If you look at any group of people who work effortlessly together, odds are the individuals share a lot in common. They might have similar backgrounds, expertise, interests, or personalities. It's only natural.

The reason? Contrary to "conventional wisdom," opposites do *not* attract.

While individuals who are different from you might initially seem intriguing, these differences will invariably push you apart in the long run. This is a scientifically proven fact. If opposites were attracted, our political system would not be the mess it is, and we would have Democrats and Republicans hugging and appreciating one another.

The fact is, opposites don't attract, they detract. They repel.

What implications does this have on business success?

Think about the people you surround yourself with at work. Are they like you? Do they think the same way? Do they have similar interests, skills, and strengths? Probably.

As a result, teams that lack diversity are the norm.

This desire for similarity has inherent advantages. When people think the same way, act the same way, speak the same way, and use the same language, things get done more quickly.

But is this ultimately good for the business?

To answer this question, consider the research of Clint Bowers and two colleagues at the University of Central Florida. They studied how the homogeneity of personalities within work groups affected performance by combining the results of thirteen studies involving five hundred teams.

At first glance, there wasn't much difference in the performance of diverse teams compared to homogeneous teams. But that wasn't the whole story. The types of tasks the teams had to perform significantly impacted performance.

Bowers and his colleagues went even further and distinguished "low-difficulty" tasks from "high-difficulty" tasks based on how much the activities involved uncertainty, complexity, and demand for high-level processing.

For relatively simple tasks, homogeneous teams consistently performed more efficiently than heterogeneous ones. When surrounded by "yes-men" and "yes-women," you agree quickly and get things done.

However, according to Bowers and his team, diverse groups consistently performed more effectively in situations involving high-difficulty tasks. That is, people who think differently could innovate better as a group.

This makes sense if you think about it. Developing something new requires a wide range of thinking. Innovation demands a diversity of perspectives, disciplines, and personalities. Having a group of people who think the same way only gives you more of the same. Having people on your team who get along well may seem easier, but it will rarely lead to new and innovative ideas.

Instead, consider the mantra: "The person you like the least is the person you need the most."

Someone different than you may, at times, seem annoying. But consider that this person is quite complementary to you. They have skills and perspectives that could provide balance and help you become more effective and innovative. They will challenge you, a crucial factor in business success.

If you only hire people who "fit the mold," you will most likely hit a growth plateau at some point. If you want to create a culture of innovation within your organization, first take stock of your current portfolio of people. Do you have a diverse mix of personality styles and divergent perspectives, or do you have a collection of like-minded professionals who will eventually limit the scope of your innovation capabilities?

If your business is creative in nature (e.g., branding or advertising), make sure you hire those with a talent for planning and managing. If your business is operational (e.g., manufacturing), ensure that you have people focused on innovation and growth.

People will naturally gravitate toward roles that fit their personality style. Look broadly across your organization. Are there varying styles that exist but are siloed within different functional areas? Is your Human Resources Department filled with empathetic communicators? Is your R & D department brimming with analytical and exacting individuals? Look for ways to cross-pollinate these groups to infuse innovation at all levels.

Additionally, consider "hiring in pairs." When at Nissan Design

International, Jerry Hirshberg would hire a free-form thinker along with someone who was more analytical. This helped ensure team diversity and the rise of uniquely creative solutions to the company's most pressing problems.

Team diversity is of extreme importance, even amongst your leadership ranks. When Sigal Barsade and colleagues at the University of Pennsylvania's Wharton business school studied top management teams at large corporations in the United States, they found that the more diverse the functional roles of the team members, the greater the average, market-adjusted financial return in those companies.

Creativity and innovation come from tension, giving rise to differing viewpoints and alternative ways of solving problems. While it may not come naturally, if you want to differentiate yourself from the competition, consider differentiating your perspective by surrounding yourself with people who think differently than you do.

 **The person you like the least is the person you need the most.**

---

*AUTHOR'S NOTE: This tip is a small slice of my larger body of work: Personality Poker®. This system is a card-based game that will create high-performing innovation teams while getting people in the right role. Go to www.personalitypoker.com to learn more. I will note that some people didn't like the title for this tip and felt I should have chosen "Hire People Who Are Not Like You." Although that statement is true, it is a different point.*

# 27

# WHY THE PYRAMIDS ARE ONE OF THE SEVEN WONDERS

M ost companies start their innovation efforts by creating a new corporate function that delivers innovation. These functions comprise employees reassigned to and dedicated to this new organization within the company. In most cases, this is a complete waste of time and money. This model keeps innovation separate from the rest of the business, and there is no involvement by the people who make critical decisions. Additionally, the innovation efforts remain out of touch with the real needs of the business.

Recognizing this common dilemma, USAA, a 22,600-employee financial service firm, took a completely different approach.

At USAA, innovation starts at the leadership level. Leadership sets the tone for the rest of the organization and is a strong advocate for innovative thinking.

Next, USAA created a "core team" comprised of thirty-five individuals, all of whom dedicate 100 percent of their time to innovation. However, here is the twist: Only ten of those individuals report directly to the innovation leadership. The other twenty-five "matrixed" individuals spend their time solely on innovation-related activities, yet with a focus on the specific innovation needs of their line of business. This creates widespread buy-in.

USAA realized that thirty-five people could not change the culture of a 22,600-person organization. Therefore, beyond the core team, they created a network of two hundred "innovation advisors," each spending 10 percent of their time on innovation efforts, working closely with the core team. In addition, there are ten "innovation champions." These leaders serve as powerful advocates for innovation and help break through any challenges that might pop up.

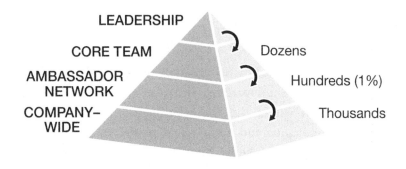

How can you use this same method to accelerate your innovation efforts?

First, ensure your leadership team is on board, as they will set the tone, demonstrate strong executive support, and help challenge the status quo.

Of course, your leadership cannot create a culture of innovation on its own as they have far too many other responsibilities. Therefore, most organizations tag someone as a full-time "innovation leader" whose role is to help shepherd the innovation process. Innovation Leaders differ from other leaders within the organization because they do not have direct responsibility over those who make innovation a reality. Ultimately, everyone in the company plays a vital role in driving innovation. The Innovation Leader is more of a mentor, coach, and negotiator than a boss or taskmaster. Their ability to influence and sell the value of innovation and its practices is paramount to their and the organization's success.

Next, create your innovation "core team" (sometimes called a center of excellence), a small cadre dedicated to driving innovation into every corner of your organization. This can indeed be a small central group in smaller companies with few geographies or lines of business. But in larger, more widely distributed organizations, the matrixed strategy is preferred as it addresses the complexities associated with geographic, product, and customer differences.

This core team has many responsibilities. Part of it involves some basics: generating awareness, building the necessary infrastructure, selecting tools, creating the training materials and plans, and developing a process for managing the innovation pipeline. But their more valuable role is serving as the eyes and ears for your innovation efforts, providing insights into the specific needs of their departments, employees, customers, vendors, and other stakeholders. They serve as advocates and mentors for innovation, bringing innovation to the masses. They are typically responsible for developing and delivering innovation/creativity training. They also run brainstorming sessions for various departments. And they play an essential role in identifying and shepherding organizational challenges. Essentially, they are the go-to people when innovation is needed.

But no core team alone can ever make innovation pervasive. The next step is to pull together your ambassador network. Although these individuals are deployed to the lines of business, they must be passionate about innovation. Often, these people dedicate as much as six hours per week (15 percent of their time) to innovation activities. This helps spread the innovation message even deeper into the organization. Since these individuals play such a critical role, contribution to innovation should be one of their performance measures.

How large should your ambassador network be? According to studies by scientist Robin Dunbar, individuals can maintain stable relationships with around 150 people. Using this capacity as a baseline for determining a maximum sphere of influence, having one person in your network for every 150 people you wish to impact (or 0.07%) would be appropriate. Still, 1 percent is a good rule of thumb. At USAA, between their Core Team and Innovation Advisors, they have almost exactly 1 percent of the organization represented.

At USAA, this approach has worked incredibly well. In only one year, they achieved 84 percent employee participation and implemented approximately one hundred employee solutions. What were the bottom-line results? There was more than ten times ROI for USAA and almost thirty times ROI for USAA members. USAA is different from shareholder companies in that it has a higher goal and motivation for caring for its members–present and former members of the military services and their families.

These are impressive results. Follow USAA's lead by embedding innovation throughout your organization.

The Egyptian pyramids worked so well because most of the weight was closer to the ground, making these structures more stable. Equally, this pyramid approach to innovation will ground your innovation efforts and fulfill the needs of the business and your customers.

 *Everyone in the company plays a role in driving innovation.*

AUTHOR'S NOTE: *This model is incredibly powerful and is what I use with my clients to scale innovation. The approach is based on work we*

*did twenty-five years ago to create a 20,000-person process and innovation practice at Accenture. We accomplished this in nine months, with the impact lasting for years. The final chapter of this book documents this approach in detail.*

# 28

# THE "TOP-DOWN" PHILOSOPHY
# SHOULD BE LEFT TO CONVERTIBLES

C harles Koch, CEO of Koch Industries, one of the most
successful companies in the world, believes that central
control is "fatal conceit" for organizations. For the past fifty years,
Koch has continually chipped away at the command-and-control
style of management. In its place, he asks employees to run their
businesses as if they owned them. When someone is brought in
specially to do a job, they are immediately given the authority to
spend money and move people when and where they choose. Decision-making within Koch is decentralized as far as possible to those
with the best local knowledge and information. This approach
must work as Koch Industries has grown more than 2,200-fold
since 1960 and is outperforming the S&P 500 by nearly 3,200
percent.

Koch Industries is involved in hazardous businesses like
asphalt, paper, pulp, oil, and gas. Therefore, several years ago, not
being satisfied with industry-average accident and injury rates, they
set a goal of moving to the top tier in the industry. Instead of having
a few safety engineers search the company for unsafe conditions,
they made safety the responsibility of every employee. Employees
were rewarded for uncovering dangerous conditions and discov-

ering new ways to conduct business more safely. This initiative resulted in 35 percent to 50 percent improvements yearly in the company's number and severity of accidents. Within one year, the company had moved from the middle of the pack to having one of the best safety records in its industry.

This simple example illustrates the value of moving decision-making from the top, down to the individuals with the best information and ability to execute. One way of making your organization more innovative is to make sure that it is structured in a way that avoids central control. This concept of pushing decision-making to the lowest levels of the organization is somewhat in vogue at the moment.

One organization that is seeking to spread this business model around the globe is WorldBlu. Traci Fenton, the founder, and CEO, calls it "organizational democracy." But unlike most traditional democracies, which conjure up thoughts of politics, bureaucracies, and a "majority rules" mentality, organizational democracy is about giving employees a voice. It is about creating the optimal conditions for learning, motivation, self-direction, and engagement.

In the past, Fenton published her "WorldBlu List of Most Democratic Workplaces" each year in the *New York Times*. In it, you would find some interesting examples of democracy in action.

At GE Aerospace, where jet engines are assembled, almost all decisions are made in consensus by teams. Whole Foods uses an open "salary book" that lists the previous year's salary and bonus for every employee by name. Semco allows employees to choose both their boss and how much they get paid. W.L. Gore has what they call a "flat lattice" approach instead of layers of hierarchy so that there is no chain of command, and the employees have direct connections to whomever they need.

Another example that Fenton shares comes from Colorado-based DaVita. With over 32,000 employees, this company provides dialysis treatments to patients suffering from chronic kidney failure. But back in 1999, the company was on the verge of bankruptcy.

The new CEO, Kent Thiry, decided that significant changes were needed. How did he do it? Rather than centralizing control in Denver, management made the radical choice of decentralizing power to the company's 1,500 clinics nationwide. By providing a clear set of parameters and giving each clinic the freedom to be its own boss within those boundaries, Thiry communicated a message of trust and respect to all the employees. Decisions are made either by consensus or by a majority vote. Every decision doesn't need to go before the entire company. Instead, those who have the best information to make decisions should make them (and that doesn't usually include the people at the top). DaVita teammates are invited each quarter to participate in a "Voice of the Village" call with the CEO and senior leadership team. The call allows employees to share information about the state of the company and address any areas of concern.

What are the results of these efforts? Operating revenues grew from $1.45 billion in 1999 to $6.1 billion in 2009, and the following year the company made the *Fortune 400*.

Innovation does not always involve new products or services. Instead, innovation can be used to help reshape your business. Innovation will organically emerge once you treat your employees as owners of the company. Although it may feel safer to control every decision, you may just control yourself out of business.

 *Central control is a fatal conceit. You may just control yourself out of business.*

---

AUTHOR'S NOTE: *Traci Fenton—a good friend of mine—has been beating the drum of organizational democracy since 1997 when she founded WorldBlu. Since the original publication of this book, she has written her own:* Freedom at Work: The Leadership Strategy for Transforming Your Life, Your Organization, and Our World *(BenBella Books, 2022).*

*In it, she highlights over fifty companies, including The WD-40 Company, DaVita, Menlo Innovations, Zappos, Pandora, Widen, HCL Technologies, and Mindvalley. If you want to dig deeper into this topic, I highly recommend her book. You can learn more here: https://www.world blu.com/freedomatworkbook.*

# 29

# USE THE REALITY TV SHOW MODEL

The Quill Corporation (a subsidiary of Staples) used a creative approach to introduce challenge-centered innovation within its organization. Using *The Apprentice* as a model, the company launched an internal competition called "The Quillionaire," in which three teams of eight competed against each other monthly. These teams were focused on solving specific business challenges, and this approach encouraged collaboration within the teams yet provided for some friendly competition.

After a month, each team presented its solutions to a panel of judges comprised of four executives. The role of the judges was to encourage participants while still challenging their solutions. The teams developed creative solutions–some of which were implemented. Everyone had a great time, and the winning team had dinner with the President at a restaurant they chose each month.

In addition to being fun, because the competitions were organized around a specific challenge, they served as a catalyst for rolling out the larger challenge-centered initiatives within the organization. The competitions were videotaped in front of a live audience and used for internal marketing.

This is one example of how a reality television show can be

used to help drive innovation. These competitions are different from the "tournaments" discussed in tip 10. These are done with employees and are as much about generating buzz and stimulating interest in innovation as they are about finding specific solutions. One side benefit of these types of competitions is that they take the pressure off "getting things right" and add some fun to the workplace. As a result, you might find solutions that are out of the ordinary.

Given the success of the Quillionaire competition, several years later, as part of its ongoing innovation efforts, Quill reintroduced the reality TV show-like concept by launching their "The BIGGEST Winner!" contest. A total of 220 individuals submitted 139 ideas, judged by a panel of Quill executives. They reviewed employee ideas in a two-stage process, beginning with an essay and expanding into a detailed executive summary along with visual presentations. Ideas were judged on their value proposition, competitive advantage, feasibility and risk, market potential/resources, and uniqueness/originality of concept.

Although this was more akin to the *American Idol* approach, the competition resulted in a junior staff member modeling a program that could potentially create a nine-million-dollar revenue stream for Quill, a sizable amount for a one-billion-dollar company. To ensure the solution's success, the company promoted the contributor, and a vice president was assigned to mentor her as she worked to make sure the idea took hold.

In these two examples, a select panel of executives determined the winners. In another instance, the competitors' peers made the final decision. A well-known electronics company holds a "county fair" each year. A huge room is set up with hundreds of booths, and all employees are encouraged to have their own booths to present new ideas. Ideas can be on anything–not necessarily even from their section of the business. In the end, the employees vote on the winners. This competition is much more about pride than a prize. To be selected by a group of peers is quite an honor.

Although the county fair is akin to using an idea-driven approach, everyone must put time and effort into fleshing out a concept and creating a physical prototype. This requires the developer to think more deeply about the concept, often leading to better results. Although people must dedicate their own time to producing stellar ideas, they are happy to do it because it taps into their true passions. As a result, it demonstrates both a greater commitment to the idea's success and encourages a more engaging process than simple virtual electronic suggestion boxes.

*The Apprentice, The Biggest Loser*, or *American Idol*. It doesn't matter which show you choose. The point is to identify ways to infuse fun, competition, and peer engagement that has your organization focused on specific and meaningful challenges. When you run these competitions, everyone comes out a winner.

> *These competitions are as much about generating buzz and stimulating interest in innovation as they are about finding specific solutions.*

---

*AUTHOR'S NOTE: This tip is based on an article I wrote for the European Business Forum back in 2005. In it, I discussed the eight levels that organizations move through on their way to an innovative culture. This is an expansion of the three levels discussed in tip 1. The levels are: 1) Ad Hoc, 2) Innovation Core Team, 3) Centre of Excellence, 4) Community of Practice, 5) Innovation Management Software, 6) Growth Engines, 7) Embedded Innovation, and 8) Organic Innovation. You can read the article here: https://stephenshapiro.com/pdfs/ebf.pdf*

# 30

# GET YOUR KNOWLEDGE WORKERS
# DOING KNOWLEDGE WORK

A t the start of my career, I worked for a large computer manufacturer. On average, I worked fifty hours a week. My direct supervisor worked sixty hours a week. Life was good until my supervisor was laid off, and I inherited all her work. Faced with having to work 110 hours a week, I decided to take a hard look at what we were doing. I discovered what many organizations would find if they did the same analysis: only a tiny percentage of their employee's time is spent on truly valuable work.

Time is a precious commodity inside organizations. There are barely enough hours in the day to do your regular job, let alone innovate on the side. How do you make time when you have none? The key to making time is to eliminate the unnecessary. Although this may seem obvious, it is rarely done in most organizations.

Throughout the weekend, I analyzed all the activities I was expected to perform. I hoped to get my work from 110 hours to 50 hours (or less). Here's what I found:

Only 20 percent of my work was high-value add. These were the high-priority items I still needed to perform.

Many activities added no value. Although we had done these

activities in the past, they were no longer necessary. I stopped doing these immediately, and no one seemed to notice.

Several activities were really the responsibility of another department or individual. Therefore, I worked to get these activities assigned to the correct parties. Not only did this reduce my workload, but it also reduced the overall time required by the company. It is always more efficient for the right person to do the right work.

Additionally, many "transactional" activities were done manually and were candidates for automation. None of these activities was particularly complicated. Therefore, I wrote some simple computer programs in a matter of hours that automated these processes.

After only two days of analysis and work, I got my workload from 110 hours to 20 hours. The point wasn't to reduce my workload. It was to make sure that I, and others, focused our energies on the activities that would have the greatest impact.

One way to make time is to get your knowledge workers doing knowledge work. For example, consider a valuable resource in most organizations: the sales representative. On average (based on my own studies), these valuable workers spend an appalling 20 percent to 35 percent of their time face-to-face with customers. The rest of the time is spent traveling, filling out forms, and sitting in meetings. This is an example of knowledge workers spending little time on valuable knowledge work. Imagine if you increased the level of knowledge work from 25 percent to 50 percent. You would, in essence, double your workforce without hiring a single person.

One notably bad example comes from a food company. Brand managers, particularly important in the food business, were spending less than 30 percent of their time on brand management, while the rest of their time went to administration, meetings, and bureaucracy.

One of the keys to helping knowledge workers focus on high-value tasks is to off-load transactional, repetitive, and administrative tasks to others (whether customers, clerks, computers, or outsourcing companies). The most significant value of technology and outsourcing is its ability to leverage an organization's assets and allow people to do more valuable work.

As another example, at the social services department in Merced County, California, most of the employees are social workers. Nevertheless, in the past, they spent almost none of their time on social work. They were busy with administrative tasks such as entering claims forms and searching manual records. Now, new systems help automate that work, freeing the social workers to do the job they were hired to do. Their overall ability to deliver services improved significantly.

Here are a few simple strategies for making more time in your day:

- What work is non-value add? Stop doing it!
- What work do you do that others *should* do? Reassign that work to the appropriate party with the best skills and authority. This will help get the work done more efficiently.
- What work do you do that others *can* do? If you are a knowledge worker, delegate or outsource your less critical activities. This will free time to focus on what matters most.
- What work can be automated? Buy off-the-shelf software to help speed things up or find someone to build you a custom solution.

Most companies recognize innovation as an essential requirement for ensuring business sustainability. Cliché as it may be, it is time to "work smarter, not harder." Focus on the genuinely value-added items that differentiate you from the competition. Eliminate, automate, or delegate the rest.

*One way to make time is to get your knowledge workers to do knowledge work.*

---

*AUTHOR'S NOTE: A little backstory on this one. After I reduced my workload from 110 hours to 20 hours, my boss called me into his office. He then proceeded to call me the laziest person he had ever met. And he meant it as a compliment. In fact, he designated me as the department's Chief Laziness Officer. My job was now to go around and find inefficiencies in the work being done and help others become more efficient. Although we hear that necessity is the mother of invention, sometimes laziness can be the father of innovation. The goal is not to "do more with less," as this is a recipe for burnout. Instead, strive to "do less and get more." Identify the leverage points of your work and focus your energies there.*

# CREATIVITY

## TECHNIQUES FOR STIMULATING CREATIVE THINKING

Innovation is an end-to-end process. Generating solutions is one of the steps in that process that requires creative thinking. To make innovation a reality, you need employees who think differently. This section contains a number of tips and techniques that can pump up their creative potential.

## 31

___

# ENCOURAGE EMPLOYEES TO GET ON THEIR SOAPBOX

I lived in London for several years and loved visiting Hyde Park's "Speaker's Corner" on Sundays. In this corner of the park, people can speak on any topic, typically about politics, religion, conspiracy theories, or alien abductions. The most compelling individuals draw a crowd. Less interesting people usually take their soapbox home early in the day.

This is a free market in action. The best speakers, as judged by the listeners, thrive while others fade away. Watching this, I realized that the Speaker's Corner concept could be a valuable technique for driving new thinking.

Consider your typical brainstorming session. Usually, one person facilitates the entire room. But this limits the discussion. Therefore, to encourage greater conversation, sometimes, these sessions break into smaller groups. The problem with this approach is that it does not allow for the cross-pollination of ideas, as people are sequestered at different tables or in other rooms.

To combat these problems, try emulating the Speaker's Corner approach. Instead of one conversation, there are many. Instead of the leader deciding what to discuss, everyone determines what is important. And people can participate in multiple discussions.

Here's how it works:

- Capture (either in the meeting or in advance) a list of topics that interest the individuals in the room. These can be based on preference, or they can be based on a pre-defined list of challenges, ideas, or solutions that are important to the organization.
- Prioritize this list down to a few critical issues. The ideal number is one topic for every eight people. For the sake of argument, let's say thirty people are participating, so you would have four topics/corners.
- Ask for volunteers - one for each topic/corner - who agree to facilitate that particular conversation. Each facilitator goes to a different "corner" with a flip chart to capture the ideas associated with their assigned topic.
- Meeting attendees can then wander freely from corner to corner as they see fit. The only rule is that everyone must either add value to a corner or receive value from a corner. If not, they should go to a different corner or create a new corner.
- Any person, at any time, can create a new corner around any topic. The new topic can be from the list, it can be an extension of an existing corner, or it can be a new topic altogether.
- Should a corner leader wish to participate in another discussion, they can recruit a new leader to continue their topic.

You will find that the most important topics with the highest energy level attract the most people. Topics that fail to draw a crowd wither on the vine (just like in Hyde Park–time to pick up the soapbox and call it a day). In one hour, you can capture more ideas than you would from a day full of meetings, and each topic benefits from the cross-pollination of ideas from all attendees.

For example, before a Speaker's Corner session with fifty participants, a client surveyed employees to determine their most pressing issues and concerns. Based on responses, they chose the most popular six topics. When people were allowed to choose which corner to go to during the event, over thirty people wanted to talk about workforce productivity. We underestimated the interest in this topic, so we took a few minutes to break the subject into subtopics, creating two additional yet slightly different corners focused on productivity. Two of the original six corners didn't attract anyone and were quickly shut down. The other conversations continued for about ninety minutes until all interested participants fully addressed all topics.

The Speaker's Corner approach allows participants to discuss what they are most passionate about. Hot topics attract a crowd, while the less popular ones are shut down. Innovate how your employees brainstorm, and you'll see an immediate difference in the quality and quantity of their conversations.

 **The Speaker's Corner concept is a useful technique for driving new thinking. It is a free market in action.**

*AUTHOR'S NOTE: This concept may feel familiar if you have experience with Open Space Technology (OST). Speaker's Corner and OST are related; however, there are subtle yet important differences. As much as I love free markets, there are times when personal agendas can derail conversations. This is why I like seeding the topics beforehand to ensure that the critical issues get addressed–at least initially. This doesn't mean that other topics can't emerge organically. They will. But starting with well-framed challenges can accelerate the process. Let's face it, this is the essence of challenge-centered innovation described in tip 4. Start with the opportunity and innovate from there.*

# 32

# THE POWER OF POSITIVE CONSTRAINTS

I n a recent client session, I had everyone in the room get into groups of two. I then pulled a brick from my briefcase and we proceeded to do the following activity:

I said, "In your pairs, I want you to go back and forth and develop a list of all the different ways you could use a brick. The first person might say, 'Put the brick under the wheels of a car to prevent it from rolling backward.' The second person might say, 'Put the brick in the toilet's tank to reduce the water used while flushing.' Then the first person might say, 'Use the brick as a replacement for the remote control when you can't find it. Throw it at the TV to turn it off.' The quality of the ideas doesn't matter. Just think freely. You have thirty seconds to develop solutions."

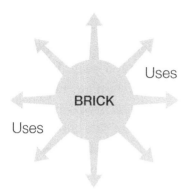

The responses ranged from using it as a paperweight to a bookend or weapon.

People generally developed their solutions by looking at the brick and considering its physical attributes: rough, heavy, and potentially dangerous. (See graphic above.) When I polled the groups for their answers, I found that most people developed similar solutions and that the range of creativity was limited.

We then played a second round.

"The question is the same," I said. "What are all of the different ways you can use a brick? But this time, instead of looking at the physical attributes of the brick, I want you to think of something random and find ways of using a brick in that situation."

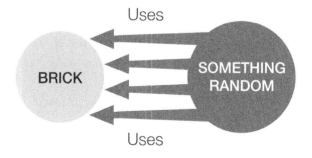

"For example," I continued, "if the random item was 'the body,' think of all the ways of using a brick on the body. You could use it as a weight to build up your biceps. You could use it as a loofah to slough off dead skin cells. You could balance it on your head to improve your posture. Or a short guy like me could attach it to the bottom of his shoes to increase his height.

"The first person in your pair will name something random. The second person will then take thirty seconds to develop as many uses of a brick for that random context. Then, you will switch, and the second person will name something random, and the first person will create a list of uses."

The difference in results was staggering. This time there was a much greater variety of solutions generated.

I have polled audiences around the world to see which approach, in their opinion, led to solutions that were more creative. Consistently, between 75 percent and 95 percent of audience members choose the second method–connect to something random–which I describe as "line thinking." I describe the first method as "dot thinking": looking at the attributes of the brick/problem and generating solutions from there.

Why do most people select the second method? Maybe it is because "line thinking" represents the true essence of creativity. Or, as Steve Jobs once said, "Creativity is just having enough dots to connect." The key word is "connect."

How do you use this concept to develop new solutions?

Choose a random object. What solutions come to mind when you think of or look at this object? What are the characteristics of this object? How can these characteristics help you solve a problem?

Where can you get ideas that stimulate this process?

- *Trends*–Identify trends and then force associations. Associations are line thinking in action. Look at industry-specific trends and more general trends. For example, how can an aging population give you an idea for a new product or service?

- *Words, expressions, and idioms*–Use a dictionary, phrase book, or quotation guide. Select a random word and see how it might stimulate a new solution.
- *Magazines*–Get a wide selection of magazines not associated with your business. Then rip out pictures, headlines, or anything that attracts your attention. Force associations and find real tangible solutions rather than fluffy platitudes.
- *Look around*–Look around the room and force associations with random items you see.

The key is to become masterful at connecting the dots.

The following few techniques are variations on the brick exercise and are designed to help develop new solutions or new applications of existing solutions.

Both ways of thinking—dot and line—are valid and useful problem-solving approaches. Both are necessary. Dot thinking tends to lead to incremental improvement ideas critical to any business for day-to-day operations, short-term growth, and traditional problem-solving. However, line thinking is the way to go when you are looking for more radical solutions that drive long-term strategic growth.

 **"Creativity is just having enough dots to connect."**— **Steve Jobs.**

---

AUTHOR'S NOTE: *I love the exercise, and I encourage you to give it a try. I've done this now with over a half million people, and the impact is powerful. But there is another point to this exercise that might be even more valuable. Too often, people say, "Think outside the box." Consider that the first way we did the exercise (no limits, no constraints) had no box, yet it yielded lower-value solutions. If you don't believe me, after doing the brick exercise the first way, ask everyone to provide their answers. Go around the room. Very quickly, you will hear repeated responses over and over. However, with the second method, you can often go through the entire room and not hear the same use mentioned twice. This tip was originally titled "The Shortest Distance Between Two Points is a Straight Line. But I felt the new title got at its essence better. The right constraints can be your friend when it comes to innovation.*

# 33

# SOMEONE ELSE HAS ALREADY SOLVED
# YOUR PROBLEM

I magine you want to create a waterproof, biodegradable adhesive that is also safe to use inside the body as a way of augmenting sutures or staples. Where would you turn? Consider the possibility that someone else might have already solved this problem. Or, in the case of the medical adhesive, *something* has already solved this problem. By studying the gecko lizard's "gravity-defying feet," researchers have developed a new type of medical adhesive with these exact properties.

The best way to quickly find solutions to your challenges is to identify someone who has already solved the problem—but in a different context. Someone from another industry, discipline, or practice might have a solution.

Previously I mentioned how a toothpaste manufacturer developed a novel concept for whitening teeth by using the same bluing agents used in laundry detergent to whiten clothes.

Another toothpaste innovation comes from GlaxoSmithKline. Their "Aquafresh iso-active" toothpaste is based on an idea from a GSK cleaning product: a gel that foams upon use, much like gel shaving creams. The toothpaste comes out like a gel but foams in

166 | BEST PRACTICES ARE STUPID

the mouth. This formulation removes 75 percent more bacteria than regular toothpaste and has proven to be a market success. All of this research about toothpaste got me thinking. If toothpaste manufacturers can find solutions from shaving cream and laundry detergent, where else could they look? To generate new concepts, I selected a few items from my house to "connect" with toothpaste:

1. *Pop Rocks:* Pop Rocks is a carbonated candy that explodes in your mouth. What if you added Pop Rock-like crystals to toothpaste? Not only would the toothpaste foam, it would fizz and explode and possibly blast the plaque off your teeth.

2. *Shampoo:* Shampoos are infused with vitamins and minerals. What if you infused toothpaste with these ingredients on top of fluoride? Or maybe you could add some homeopathic remedies? Additionally, sublingual administration (under the tongue) is a common and effective way of delivering drugs directly into the bloodstream and might be helpful for those who don't like taking pills.

3. *Conditioner:* We use shampoo to clean and conditioner to protect. What if they created a tooth conditioner, a special toothpaste that you use after your regular toothpaste? It could coat your teeth to prevent staining, bad breath, or split ends. What if you created a "leave in" conditioner where toothpaste is applied but not spit out, and it could keep working all day? Even better, they could borrow the "technology" used by shampoos like Pert Plus, which combines shampoo and conditioner into one formulation.

4. *Moisturizers:* Several moisturizers have an A.M. and a P.M. formulation. One is used in the morning and the other at night before sleep. The A.M. formula of

toothpaste could be infused with caffeine that would be absorbed into the bloodstream sublingually. And the P.M. formulation could be infused with melatonin to help you sleep better at night.

5. *Weight Loss Products:* What if you could create toothpaste that reacts with certain unhealthy foods, making them taste bad? This might cause you to reduce the amount of food you eat. Or what if you created a toothpaste with an appetite suppressant?

Of course, the ultimate answer might involve a product that eliminates the need for brushing altogether.

This exercise aims to bring us to one of the most useful questions in the world of creativity: "Who else has solved this problem?"

When you ask this question, you may quickly find a solution to your challenge. To find solutions from other industries, processes, products, or disciplines, ask the following questions:

- What is the problem you want to solve (e.g., How can we make teeth whiter without abrasives or bleaches?)?
- What is a more "abstract" way to frame the problem (e.g., How can we make something that is already white even whiter?)?
- Who else addresses a similar problem (e.g., laundry detergents that use bluing agents)?
- How could you adapt their solution to your problem (e.g., create a toothpaste with a blue die in the middle)?

How has this concept been used in the real world?

A gas pipeline company developed a new technology for finding and sealing pipeline cracks by mirroring the clotting agents in the human body.

A boat rental company uses a Netflix-like subscription model. Netflix allows you to receive unlimited DVDs each month, but you can only have a certain number (depending on your subscription level) in your possession at any given time. The boat company offers members unlimited access to several boats with two open reservation slots at any given time. As soon as you use one reservation, you get another.

A company was looking for a better way to diagnose computer crashes. They wanted to be able to replay the crash to recreate the problem. Who solved a similar problem? TiVo, the digital video recorder (DVR). The idea came about when inventor Jonathan Lindo asked, "Wouldn't it be great if we could just TiVo this and replay it?" As a result, he and Jeff Daudel created ReplayDIREC-TOR. This tool records all of your activities, letting you replay them later to help diagnose computer crashes, much like TiVo. The company that developed this technology was purchased by CA Technologies in 2012, which was then acquired by Broadcom in 2018.

Solutions can come from anywhere.

Sometimes the best solutions already exist inside your own organization. In innovation parlance, sharing ideas across business units and brands is called "convergence." For many organizations, such as Johnson & Johnson, this is one of the most critical components of their innovation program. You just need to frame the question correctly to identify the most appropriate product line, function, division, or brand where this problem has already been solved.

And, of course, in some cases, the best solutions will come from outside your company or even outside the world of business.

Where will your next significant innovation come from?

 *The most helpful question in the world of creativity is: "Who else has solved this problem?"*

*AUTHOR'S NOTE: I find asking "Who else...?" to be a potent tool for solving problems and identifying new opportunities. A story I love comes from an annual event called Pumps and Pipes. A group of cardiologists get together with people from the oil/gas pipeline industry and share what they know about the cardiovascular system and how it could apply to the transmission of oil/gas, and vice versa. What these two industries share in common is that they both solve problems around fluids moving through tubes. The solutions that can come from collaborations like this are amazing. For example, pipeline filters are used to reduce sludge in oil fields. Adapting this solution, cardiologists built a device to filter blood clots (essentially sludge in the veins) from the venous system. The result is the Greenfield inferior vena cava filter, a breakthrough in reducing pulmonary embolisms.*

# 34

---

# ADAPT YOUR PRODUCT TO A
# DIFFERENT ENVIRONMENT

Although label maker manufacturers primarily sell their products through office supply stores, their uses are unlimited. To expand its reach, one such manufacturer made a list of two hundred possible customer segments: hospitals, authors, farmers, computer technicians, tollbooth collectors, or hotel concierges. Then each day, they would choose one from the list and develop a list of possible marketing opportunities. Although sometimes a slight product adaptation was needed, in many cases, it was simply a matter of changing the marketing materials.

The previous tips were about creating new products. But sometimes, the best innovation is taking something already existing and adapting it to a new environment. How might you sell your products/services to a different customer market than usual? Make a random list of potential targets and "force" an association between your existing product and that market's needs. Then find ways of marketing and packaging your product to meet those needs.

How can you take a product that has no market potential and turn it into a cash cow? Consider Arm & Hammer. Baking soda is a commodity. And because few people bake from scratch anymore, getting people to buy more baking soda for baking is a losing proposition. What do you do? Find new uses. Arm & Hammer turned their simple baking soda into an empire of product extensions. Refrigerator fresheners made of 100 percent baking soda, supported with clever packaging. Carpet fresheners are made up of nearly 100 percent baking soda, enhanced with a mild fragrance. Laundry wash booster, toothpaste, pot and pan cleaners, polishes, and more. The company took a simple product and extended it in previously unimaginable ways.

Although it is not always advisable to stray too far from your core audience or product, adaptive innovation can sometimes provide an extra revenue boost without investing heavily in new products.

 *Sometimes the best innovation is taking something existing and adapting it to a new environment.*

AUTHOR'S NOTE: *This message goes particularly well with the "brick" exercise in tip 32. Connecting your product or service to different contexts (e.g., the different customer segments the label maker identified) can be a great way to find new insights.*

# 35

# DON'T PUT THE "NO" IN INNOVATION

I mprovisational comedy is a great creativity training tool. The great improv comedian Neil Mullarkey (yes, that's his real name) once taught me an improvisational game where the objective is to tell a story, one person at a time, without ever saying "yeah, but."

This relates to innovation because so many people put the "no" in inNOvation. New ideas are often met with the immediate response, "Yeah, but," followed by a dozen reasons why the idea won't work—we don't have enough money, there is not enough time, it's suitable for someone else but not us. Instead, use the improv comedy technique where you build on the ideas of others using the words "Yes, and" while eliminating "Yeah, but" from your vocabulary.

Try this game the next time you have a problem to solve, like inventing the next hot design for your product. Have one person throw out the first idea and continue, "Yes, and...," building on the previous idea. The key is to answer quickly and avoid overthinking. Top-of-head answers tend to tap into a part of the brain we don't use during our usual thinking process. Be sure that your answer is a contribution. It should build on what the previous person said rather than invalidate it. You will develop many new ideas throughout the play. Many of the ideas will be duds. Don't worry! Play with it. Have fun. You never know when you will find a real gem. After all, it is only a game. Over time, this will become a normal mode of operating. You will become the master at breakthrough thinking regularly by building on the ideas of others. Sir Isaac Newton once said, "If I have seen further, it is only by standing on the shoulders of giants."

Of course, while fleshing out ideas, concerns will surface that need to be addressed. You can't just sweep these "yeah, buts" under the rug. In these situations, learn to phrase these concerns as challenges. For example, when brainstorming, inevitably, someone will say, "We don't have enough time to implement this idea," or "We don't have enough money." Instead, state this concern as a challenge, such as "How can we get more money?" Or "How can we do this for less money?" Once you define a new challenge, you can use any of these creativity techniques to find new solutions.

Practice doing this every day. If you struggle with breaking the "yeah but" mentality, put a jar in your home or office. Any time you or others say, "Yeah, but," put a dollar in the pot to help raise awareness and deter the voicing of these negative reactions to your (and their) ideas. It is a fun, non-threatening way of providing feedback to your peers. Use the money to take improv training classes.

 **One improvisational game requires participants to tell a story, one person at a time, without ever using the words "yeah, but."**

---

AUTHOR'S NOTE: *As mentioned previously, when we discussed failure, I have moved away from worrying about yeah but. What concerns me more is, "Wow, this is a great idea." Loving your ideas can lead to confirmation bias, increasing your risk of failure. I wrote an article about it here: https://stephenshapiro.com/brilliant-ideas-that-stink/.* Having said *that, I am a fan of improvisational comedy and highly recommend a new book by my friend Neil Mullarkey:* In the Moment: Build Your Confidence, Communication and Creativity at Work *(Kogan Page, 2023).*

## 36

---

# HOW CAN YOU MAKE THE IMPOSSIBLE POSSIBLE?

M agicians are master innovators. They make the impossible possible. They decide, "Hey, I want to slice a person in half," and then they find a way to do it without killing the subject.

In this, there is a valuable lesson for creative thinking.

Sometimes we get stuck in the mundane. We get stuck in thinking about what's real and what we believe is possible.

But what if you could become masterful at making the seemingly impossible possible? What if, instead of solving possible challenges, you started to solve seemingly impossible ones? What if, instead of looking for realistic solutions to challenges, you began with impractical ones?

When solving problems, we typically attempt to move from point A (where we are today) to point B (where we want to go). But often, we fall short and end up at A' (as depicted in the graphic).

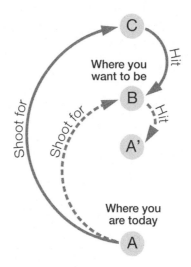

However, if we shoot for point C (the seemingly impossible), even if we fall short, we might just hit point B.

When solving a problem, a useful question is, "What are impossible or impractical solutions?" This question will stretch your thinking. From there, you can figure out ways to make these impractical solutions practical.

To encourage this kind of thinking, try this technique. It can be done in pairs or with small groups. It is done in a few simple steps.

STEP 1: Make sure you have a clearly defined opportunity/challenge statement. Example: "How might we promote our new internet-based business?"

STEP 2: Have one person give an outrageous solution. I typically suggest that if it is not "illegal, immoral, or impossible," it is probably not wild enough. Example: "Rearrange the stars in the sky to spell out our website address."

. . .

**STEP 3:** Have the other person (or people) list three attributes they like about that solution. Example: (a) Everyone worldwide can see it; (b) It is permanent; (c) It doesn't adversely impact the environment.

**STEP 4:** Next, have the other person (or people) list three things that would improve the solution. Example: (a) Have it be visible twenty-four hours a day, not just a night; (b) Design it such that you don't have to look up to see it; (c) Create a concept such that people won't have to remember or write down the website address.

**STEP 5:** Finally, use the attributes identified in steps 3 and 4 to either refine the original solution or develop different ones. Examples: Attribute 4(a) (visible twenty-four hours a day) may lead to the website address being displayed in lights in Times Square, New York City. Or, "twenty-four hours a day" and "stars" may get you thinking about movie stars and how they might promote your business. Or attribute 3(b) (make it permanent) may get you thinking about other permanent things, such as tattoos. What if you created a nicely designed temporary rub-on tattoo? Or got nightclub owners to stamp your web address on the hands of people as they enter?

This approach works well because step 2 allows you to think without constraints. Step 3 "validates" the original solution and the person who generated it. And steps 4 and 5 make the solution practical.

Instead of just going for what seems practical, shoot for the seemingly impossible... and make it possible.

> *What if you could become masterful at making the seemingly impossible possible? What if, instead of looking for realistic solutions to challenges, you started with solutions that seemed impractical?*

---

*AUTHOR'S NOTE: When done correctly, this activity is extremely powerful. I remember one event where two people walked out in the middle of the exercise. When they returned, they told the group that they'd been working on a problem for six months with no solution. Within five minutes of doing this exercise, they found a solution they had never considered. This is the power of magic. I've always loved magic. For me, it went beyond entertainment; it was an intellectual endeavor. I enjoyed trying to figure out how an illusion was done. The actual solution didn't matter because it was the process of thinking about the effect that I liked. When I was younger, there was a TV show called* Breaking the Magician's Code. *Each week, the "masked magician" revealed how some popular tricks were done. On the show, he first performed the illusion as the audience would see it. Then he would do the trick again, showing how it was done. I would watch the show and pause after he performed it the first time, before the reveal. I would then write down all of the different ways I thought he could have done the trick. Only after I had at least one solution would I watch how it was done. It's a great exercise to get your brain thinking about how to make the impossible possible.*

# 37

## STAND IN SOMEONE ELSE'S SHOES

Think back to the last time you bought a car. What did you notice as you drove your shiny new vehicle off the lot? Did you notice that everyone else seemed to be driving the same car? Obviously, the number of cars like yours on the road did not increase overnight. Instead, by changing the "filter" in which you view the world, you change how it appears to you.

Because we can only see the world through the filter we have built up over time, the only way to change perspectives is to change the filter. Unfortunately, it is difficult to "see" the filter you are using. Sometimes it is easier to replace your existing filter with a new one.

Try this. Each morning when you wake up, make believe you are someone different. Pretend you are a detective, a mechanic, an artist, or a gardener. It really doesn't matter whom you choose to be. You will then begin to see, hear, or experience things that you have never before. By focusing on different elements, you will begin to have new perspectives.

You can also use this concept more analytically during brainstorming sessions. To do this, use the following steps:

- Identify the person you want to emulate. You can do this randomly. Or, you can consider people from entirely different disciplines who have solved related problems. What are their primary characteristics? For example, you may choose Walt Disney, known for creating magical experiences.
- Next, ask, "How would this person solve this problem?" If you were to hire them as a consultant to your organization, what would they suggest? Disney might encourage you to redesign your customer experience to be more engaging, even when they are waiting in a queue.

Creativity requires us to see the world with fresh eyes. Unfortunately, it is difficult to overcome ingrained perspectives and habitual thinking. By standing in someone else's shoes, we can see the world through their eyes, offering us different vantage points.

 *Each morning when you wake up, make believe you are someone different.*

AUTHOR'S NOTE: *I love the simplicity of this technique and the fact that it can be done anywhere at any time. It allows you to focus on specific elements of your environment. The filter doesn't need to be a person; it can be a sensory trait, a concept, or anything that will inspire you. If you get stuck for ideas, here is a list to get you started:*

- Hear: *music, harmony, dance, your favorite musician*
- See: *art, architecture, your favorite artist*
- Think: *science, research, experimentation, a genius*
- Feel: *emotions, dreams, pleasure, fears*
- Taste: *smell, flavors, your favorite chef*

- Performance: *directing, movies, your favorite actor*
- Laughter: *improvisation, your favorite comedian*
- Speed: *racing, an auctioneer, a turtle*
- Fun: *play, games, sports, your favorite athlete*
- Magic: *illusion, misdirection, your favorite magician*
- Books: *words, mystery, your favorite author*
- Design: *brand, promote, a marketing director*
- Stakeholders: *customers, employees, suppliers, shareholders, partners, regulators*
- Trust: *friends, family, your favorite teacher, your spouse*

## 38

# INNOVATION IS CHILD'S PLAY

I remember watching two young boys playing outside. They wore bed sheets fashioned into capes. The first boy started by making his fingers into a gun, pointing it at the other boy, and saying, "I'm zapping you with my laser beam." The second boy said, "That's okay because I am wearing my mirrored suit, so the laser is bouncing back at you." And the play continued for hours, going back and forth between the two children until it was time for lunch.

The concept of play and games can be a useful tool for enhancing creativity. They make work more fun, reduce stress, and get people involved in the action. However, not all games are created equally. The games adults play are certainly not child's play.

The games adults play have rigid rules, an ending, and winners and losers. Think about it: Monopoly, poker, or basketball. These activities all have complex rules that the players must adhere to. If you break the rules, you "go to jail," are disqualified, or get penalized. And these games have a well-defined ending. Play is over when all the other players are out of money when the "clock" says there's no more time, or when everyone has had their turn. And nearly every adult game has a winner and one or more losers. They are competitions. Although these games can be fun, they tend to create a focus on winning.

Contrast this with the way kids play. They have very loose rules, they play until they say it ends, and there is no concept of winner/loser. Kids make up the rules as they go along. They improvise. Even universal rules don't apply to kids. They can don a cape and fly through the air, defying the laws of gravity. Rarely is a stopwatch involved. Children simply play until they get tired of that game. And then they invent a new game. The only clocks involved with kids' games are the watches on the wrists of their parents.

When children play, there are no winners or losers. Yes, they might have battles with imaginary swords or superpowers. And some victims get hurt or die in the heat of battle, but they come back as a new character. The game does not end with the death of a player.

Adult games can limit creativity. The rules, deadlines, and pressure prevent a flow of new ideas. They create stress.

If you want to enhance creativity, passion, and productivity, I encourage you to play like kids. These timeless, unbounded, and rule-free games can create an environment of free-flowing thinking. Studies show that 98 percent of five-year-olds test as highly creative, yet only 2 percent of adults do. We don't lose our creativity; we learn habits that stop it from emerging.

How does this apply to your organization?

I'm not suggesting that you go out and buy a foosball table or Nerf balls. Instead, find ways to stretch the imagination. One way to do this is to view lofty goals as a game rather than a stress-inducing end goal.

Imagine a company with a target of doubling its business over the next five years. That equates to a 14 percent growth rate each year (assuming compounding). Most companies, with hard work and some creative thinking, could hit those numbers, though it would certainly not be easy.

Because a 14 percent growth rate is viewed as doable, it might create a confident expectation in the minds of the executives and employees. This is an adult game. It becomes competitive, and you (the individual or the organization) either win or lose.

But what if the organization targets growing by 50 percent a year? That level of growth is unprecedented, and it would certainly stretch the way employees think. A 14 percent improvement can most likely be attained through conventional thinking. But a 50 percent growth target would require a breakthrough.

It might also have an interesting psychological impact on the organization. Because a 50 percent growth rate is unheard of, especially for a well-established large corporation, no one in the organization would expect that outcome. Surely the top executives would not expect employees to deliver on those targets.

As a result, the 50 percent target becomes a "game." As long as everyone in the organization believes they are playing a game designed to energize them and is not designed explicitly around hitting the target, people will naturally become more motivated. This, in turn, will stimulate creativity. Even if the company does not hit 50 percent growth rates, it will certainly have a better chance of hitting the 14 percent improvement than if it focused on that as the end goal.

In the words of Michelangelo, "The greater danger for most of us is not that our aim is too high and we miss it, but that it is too low and we hit it."

 *"The greater danger for most of us is not that our aim is too high and we miss it, but that it is too low and we hit it." —Michelangelo.*

---

AUTHOR'S NOTE: *This tip is based on an article I wrote over twenty years ago while observing children play in Hyde Park in London. It inspired me because I realized that as we got older, we lost the ability to play for the sake of play. Since the publication of this book in 2011, Simon Sinek wrote his book The* Infinite Game *(Penguin Portfolio, 2019. The premise is similar. If you want to explore this topic further, that might be a good book to add to your reading list.*

## 39

## SOMETIMES IT'S LOGICAL TO BE ILLOGICAL

S ome of the most creative ideas come from the most unnatural combinations. Imagine a "slot machine" that facilitates illogical combinations of "who, what, where, when, how, and how much" parameters. When you pull the handle, random combinations are generated.

For example, if you are tasked with redesigning the supermarket checkout process, you might look at the "who," "where," and "when" parameters.

- "Who" options might be the cashier, the customer, a random employee, or no one.
- "Where" options might be at the cash register, on the shelf, in the shopping cart, at home, or at the exit.
- "When" options might be while placing the item in the cart, after making all purchases, or before making purchases.

The typical combination for supermarket checkout is that it is done by the cashier (who), at the cash register (where), and after all of the purchases are made (when).

When you spin the wheels of the slot machine, you might get some random combinations like the following:

- *Random Option 1:* The customer (who) scans as they make their purchases (when) on their shopping cart (where). Several supermarkets now use this checkout system whereby customers can scan their items as they go with a handheld scanner.
- *Random Option 2:* Scanning is done at the exit (where) by no one (who) after making all the purchases. To make this option work, RFID technology could scan all groceries via radio as the person leaves. If the shopper has an RFID tag on their keychain linked to a credit card on file, scanning of individual items could be eliminated.
- *Random Option 3:* The customer (who) scans at home (where) before making purchases (when). If customers have a scanner attached to their trashcan, they can scan the barcodes after a product is used when they throw out the empty package. This could trigger an automatic replenishment for home delivery.

You get the idea. The possibilities are endless. Although many combinations may be duds, the payoff can be huge when you get a winner – just like a slot machine.

And you don't need to build a slot machine. You can list the different options for each parameter and then randomly select one from each column.

| WHO | WHEN | WHERE |
|---|---|---|
| Cashier | After Purchase | At the Checkout Counter |
| Customer | Before Purchase | At the Point of Food Pickup |
| Floor Walker | During Purchase | On the Shopping Cart |
| Automated Technology | Before Going to the Store | At Another Location |
| Someone Else | After Leaving the Store | At the Customer's Home |
| No One | After Using the Product | At the Exit |

Using this approach is a great way to uncover implicit assumptions about the business. When you generate combinations different from those done in the past, people will almost surely say, "Hey, we can't do that because..." You then begin to uncover the underlying assumptions. This is where real innovation can emerge. Illogical combinations can lead to genuinely logical solutions.

 *Illogical combinations can lead to genuinely logical solutions.*

*AUTHOR'S NOTE: This tip was initially published in my first book, 24/7 Innovation: A Blueprint for Surviving and Thriving in an Age of Change (McGraw-Hill, 2001). The content was something we developed at Accenture back in 1998. At that time, the self-checkout concept didn't exist. And Amazon Go (similar to Random Option 2 above) wasn't even a consideration because Amazon was only an online bookstore back then. We were ahead of our time when we did this work. In fact, we built a digital slot machine. Here's a picture of it.*

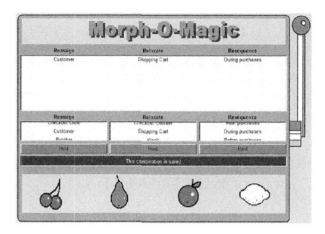

# 40

# PREDICT WHAT THE COMPETITION
# WILL DO NEXT

On December 22. 2001, Richard Reid was caught with plastic explosives in the soles of his shoes. That's why we must walk barefoot through airports while our shoes are scanned. On August 9, 2006, two dozen people were arrested in the UK because they plotted to bring liquid explosives on planes leaving Heathrow Airport. As a result, we now have to travel with miniature shampoos, shaving creams, and toothpaste.

Enron had its meltdown. What was done in response? Stringent rules like the Sarbanes-Oxley Act were implemented. When our financial institutions started to falter, seven hundred billion dollars of the taxpayers' money was spent to sort out the mess.

These are examples of a "reactionary" approach to innovation. Wait for something to happen and then try to devise a response.

Most organizations use creativity to help them determine what to do next based on current information. They brainstorm ideas, select the best solutions, and implement the most promising ones. Creativity is used to determine what *your organization* will do next.

But in these rapidly changing times, creativity can be even more valuable for determining what the *marketplace and your competitors* will do next. Or, if you are the government, it may help determine what your banks and terrorists will do next.

When did you last have a brainstorming session where you asked the following questions?

- What are we most afraid our competition will do to us?
- Who is not a competitor now but might be in the future?
- What shift might happen in the buying habits of our customers that may make our product/service less appealing?
- How can a sagging economy help our business?
- What emerging products or services may make our business irrelevant?

The list of outside-in questions can be endless–and valuable. In your next brainstorming session, try the following:

- Brainstorm your list of questions, building on mine above.
- Determine which ones you want to tackle first.
- Brainstorm, using a variety of creativity techniques, to identify "possible" outcomes.
- For those deemed plausible, brainstorm a list of "triggers" for each. These are market conditions that tell you that the given scenario is moving from "possible" to "plausible."
- Set up a corporate "radar" system to help monitor external conditions. Have everything in place such that you can implement critical ideas when market conditions dictate.

This approach blends creativity with scenario-based planning. It helps you move from reactive solutions to proactive solutions.

And in today's volatile world, this might be the key to your long-term survival.

 **In these rapidly changing times, creativity can be even more valuable for determining what the marketplace and your competitors will do next.**

---

*AUTHOR'S NOTE: Since the beginning of time, futurists have been trying their best to guess what the future holds. Sure, they've gotten it right sometimes, but they've also missed the mark on other occasions. That said, the whole point of this exercise isn't to find one surefire prediction of the future but rather to imagine a bunch of different ways things could go. Some of these scenarios might happen, others might not. By thinking about all these different outcomes, we can hedge our bets, spreading our choices and investments across different possibilities.*

# CULTURE

SCALING INNOVATION

# HOW WE CREATED A 20,000-PERSON INNOVATION PRACTICE AT ACCENTURE IN NINE MONTHS

Back in 1996, I was asked to create an innovation capability within the consulting firm Accenture (then Andersen Consulting). The goal was to help our process and software experts to focus more on value creation through a collective mindset shift.

In the end, all 20,000 members of the process competency group (the largest group within Accenture at that time) were trained in our new philosophy: Process Excellence Principles (PEP). It was a huge success; it became one of the highest-rated programs in the company's history. The process only took nine months, from the initial concept to training all 20,000 people—and the results lasted for years. Since then, I've used this model with other clients with equal success.

Although the overall strategy is similar to a traditional train-the-trainer approach, the key to sustainability involved creating a series of support structures that ensured long-term acceptance and application.

By adjusting this approach to meet your specific needs, an organization of any size could find the same success that we found at Accenture. You will notice some overlap in this section with the content from tip 27.

## THE OVERALL MODEL

Before we look at the steps, we must first understand the general philosophy we used. This is the same model I use with my clients to this day. The following figure displays the strategy I employ. As you can see, it applies both a top-down and bottom-up process, where experts mentor less-experienced individuals while allowing everyone to graduate to the next level of mastery.

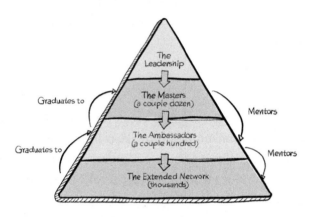

The **Leadership** comprises the top leaders of your organization. Although they may not be actively involved, they must be aligned with the goals and process to understand and buy into the overall strategy.

The **Masters** include a small group of individuals who learn the methods, apply them to real-world opportunities, and gain true mastery. They participate in an intensive program that allows them to practice and apply various skills. These individuals would support and mentor the levels below them. Although several hours a week are invested, this is not a full-time position as they continue to conduct their daily responsibilities.

The next level down is **the Ambassadors**. These individuals provide broader support to the rest of the organization. Although they develop skills in innovation, they don't have the same level of expertise as the Masters. These are the trainers. Their time investment is typically a few hours a month as the skills-building activities were not as extensive as The Masters.

**The Extended Network** refers to the rest of the organization— as deep and wide as you want. Many will participate in the one-day training program and not receive further training. Others may wish to continue to engage more deeply.

With this process as a backdrop, let's consider the steps for delivering this culture change.

## STEP 1: DEVELOP THE DELIVERY PLAN

The first step involves having clear goals and objectives. What would success look like? How would it be measured? Although success was partly measured by education, the real impact was from application, value creation, and sustainability. How can we create more value for our clients so that they want to continue working with us?

To achieve these goals, we identified approximately two hundred consultants from our workforce around the world who already had some level of expertise in this topic of innovation; then, we leveraged them to drive the culture change. These were the Ambassadors. They not only trained others in our PEP approach, but they also became critical leaders of innovation on consulting projects.

If your organization is smaller (or larger), you can adjust the numbers accordingly so that the Ambassadors represent about 1 percent of your organization. Why 1 percent? According to studies by scientist Robin Dunbar, individuals can maintain stable relationships with around 150 people (called Dunbar's Number). Using this capacity as a baseline for determining a maximum sphere of influence, having one person in your network for every 150 people you wish to impact (or 0.07%) would be appropriate. Still, 1 percent is a good rule of thumb.

At Accenture, we were fortunate because we already had a skill base that we could build on. We identified these two hundred individuals knowing that, with some training, they could provide a powerful delivery.

Most organizations, however, don't have as much experience with innovation, so a modified approach is typically required. Not to worry: there are many ways to develop a group of experts who support the program. For your organization, instead of selecting people based solely on their content expertise, consider identifying Ambassadors who are passionate and interested in innovation. Also, choosing people who are dynamic and engaging is a bonus. Their expertise can be developed later with the support of your Masters.

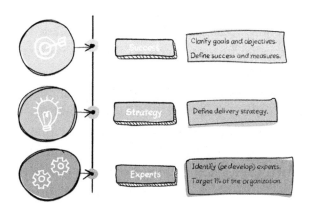

## STEP 2: DEVELOP CONTENT

Once our overall strategy was set, our next step involved creating the content. This included the entire methodology, a one-day PEP training program, a three-day train-the-trainer (T3) workshop, a full-length PEP book, a quick reference card, and other materials.

Because Accenture started with a blank sheet, we needed to assemble a dedicated team to complete the work. Fortunately, there are many sources of innovation content these days. For example, my clients are given access to my entire library of videos, tools, templates, books, and methodologies, all customized to meet specific company needs.

**Pro tip:** For the one-day PEP training program, we included a series of short videos to use at specific points to ensure that critical concepts were consistently delivered. For your training, be sure you have someone dynamic recorded on these videos, as they will be the program's backbone. In addition to providing key messages, these videos can also help increase the energy in the training session—and take some pressure off the trainers.

## STEP 3: TRAIN THE MASTERS

At Accenture, besides the Ambassadors, who ran the training sessions, we decided to nurture a smaller group of individuals (about two dozen) who exhibited mastery of innovation: the Masters. This group would provide deeper support so the Ambassadors always had someone to turn to within the organization for guidance. Since Accenture is a consulting firm, we found those individuals with relative ease; with our new materials, they only needed some light training to reach the desired level of mastery.

Most companies aren't as fortunate. Therefore, before you train the trainers (aka the Ambassadors), I highly recommend that you create a group of individuals who have or can quickly gain mastery in the content—not just general knowledge, not just the ability to deliver a training course. These people should have a deep understanding of the content and be able to apply the principles of it.

For Accenture's organization of 20,000 with two hundred Ambassadors, we identified about twenty individuals who would ultimately become Masters. This amounts to about 0.1% of the organization, or one Master for every ten Ambassadors. This ratio ensures the required depth of understanding among a few who can provide long-term support to the rest of the organization.

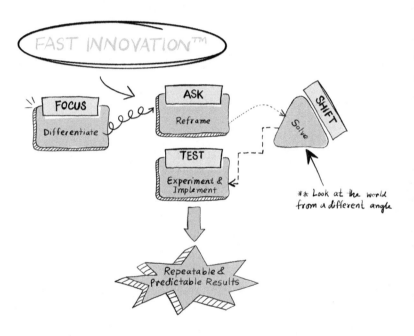

### STEP 4: TRAIN THE TRAINERS

Next, at Accenture, all two hundred Ambassadors participated in a three-day train-the-trainer (T3) workshop. These workshops were designed to help them deliver the one-day PEP training to the Extended Network. As the Ambassadors were located worldwide, I conducted four T3 sessions on four continents. This minimized the travel requirements of the participants.

By the end, each "trainer" felt they had the skills to deliver the one-day program successfully. To further reinforce the content, the Masters were present at the T3 sessions to support the Ambassadors, fielding any questions and reviewing concepts.

Determine the best locations for your organization to conduct the sessions and who should lead them. When clients work with me, I personally lead all the T3 workshops so that there is consistency across the globe. However, you may choose to have your Masters conduct these sessions.

Regardless of who runs the T3 sessions, you would assign two Masters to a group of twenty Ambassadors. As the cultural shift moves forward, this will allow for deeper support with a smaller, tighter community.

2 MASTERS PER
10 TRAINERS

MASTERS

**STEP 5: ROLL OUT**

After training the Ambassadors, it was time to deliver the content to all 20,000 people. At Accenture, each daylong PEP training session was delivered by two trainers (Masters and/or Ambassadors). Each trainer signed up to do several sessions.

As we were a geographically dispersed company, typically, the sessions were organized based on geography. However, in some cases, they were delivered based on the industry or operating group. The training sessions were usually limited to fifty to one hundred participants. We conducted over 250 sessions around the world over several months.

For your organization, determine the best strategy for delivering the content. Is it by business unit, where people from the same team are trained simultaneously, regardless of geography? Or maybe it is by location, even if the people are from different groups. Ideally, you would decide in Step 1: Develop the Delivery Plan.

**STEP 6: CREATE SUPPORT STRUCTURES**

Within nine months, we delivered the training to all 20,000 people.

We knew, however, that a one-day training session would not be sufficient to change a culture. Therefore, in addition to the training, we wrote a book that was distributed to all attendees (40,000 were distributed in total, including clients and other consultants at Accenture). We also created a brief pocket reference guide. These were distributed to attendees at the sessions. In addition, we created an online library of resources to provide further support.

Equally important (if not more important), we also created several communities that provided ongoing support:

MASTERS NETWORK: To help the Masters continue building their skills and dealing with any larger issues, we created a community just for them. We had regular in-person meetings and used online collaboration tools. Now, of course, meetings can be conducted virtually.

AMBASSADORS NETWORK: The Ambassadors also had their own community. The Masters directly supported it. Given Dunbar's Number, this is a critical group as it represents a critical mass of individuals who have enough sphere of influence to impact all 20,000. Deepening their skills, providing support, and building camaraderie is essential for continuing momentum and ensuring the long-term success of your culture change. Again, there were in-person meetings and online collaboration tools. Occasionally, I also delivered deep-dive workshops to the entire group.

COMMUNITY OF INTEREST: Some individuals from within The Extended Network (the 20,000 people who received the PEP training) wanted to continue learning beyond the one-day program. For this self-selected group, we created a Community of Interest. The Masters and the Ambassadors supported this. Although the group was relatively informal, it did help keep the conversation alive. Occasionally, I delivered a high-level speech to the group, sometimes at large Accenture-wide gatherings. And over time, some of these individuals chose to delve deeper into the content and become Ambassadors.

. . .

Keeping the conversation going is the key to long-term success and a true culture change. Raise concerns. Address challenges. Share new insights. Build momentum. Share successes.

For your organization, create similar communities to help the conversations continue and thrive. Also, create an online portal with resources such as videos, books, templates, tools, cheat sheets, and more. This will give people access to the latest updates and helpful information.

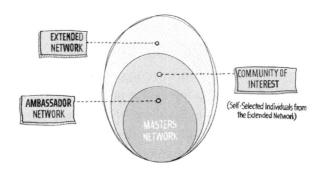

**BOTTOM LINE**

After five years of watching the program run successfully, I left Accenture to start my own business and apply the same techniques to a broader range of companies. When I left, the impact was still noticeable. I continue to meet people twenty-five years later who remember the program and can recite the critical lessons from the content. That's impact.

The model described above built incredible momentum around the content and the continuing conversations. The key is to look at this not as a training program but as a cultural shift that takes on a life of its own.

When you blend this proven model with proven content, you can bring the power of innovation to any organization of any size.

We've used this model successfully at numerous other companies, including organizations in office supplies, pharmaceuticals, manufacturing, consumer goods, and financial services.

———

How can you develop people with deep mastery? My clients use my FAST Innovation® Mastery Program (please visit **https://stephenshapiro.com/mastery** to learn more). This is a powerful and cost-effective way to engage people in your organization at all levels: the Masters, the Ambassadors, and the Extended Network.

# CONTINUE THE JOURNEY

Thank you for reading to the end of this book. However, this doesn't have to be the end of our journey together. You can delve deeper into my work on innovation in many ways.

## OTHER BOOKS AND PRODUCTS

*Invisible Solutions®: 25 Lenses that Reframe and Help Solve Difficult Business Problems* (Amplify Publishing, 2020). When *Best Practices Are Stupid* was first published, many readers expressed curiosity about tip 4. They asked, "How can we create a better box?" *Invisible Solutions* answers that question. It offers the methodology and tools needed for reframing any problem, paving the way for better solutions. Learn more at www.invisiblesolutionsbook.com

*Pivotal* (Amplify Publishing, 2024). Although *Pivotal* has not yet been published, I felt it essential to mention it here as it is a vital book for innovators. While *Invisible Solutions* equips you to tackle almost any business problem, *Pivotal* gives you laser focus on which problems are worth solving. It provides tools and frameworks for prioritizing your innovation investments, shedding light on what matters most. It's time to stop the perpetual pivoting and spinning in circles. Instead, get clarity on which endeavors will make the greatest impact and help you become irreplaceable to your customers. This is the key to becoming pivotal. Learn more at www.thepivotalbook.com

***Goal-Free Living: How to Have the Life You Want NOW!*** (Wiley, 2005). Although it's not strictly a book on innovation, it was written to introduce innovation techniques to personal lives. I traveled across the United States and interviewed 150 creative individuals. During this three-month trip, I discovered that these individuals had a distinct approach to goals compared to others. I truly believe this book has the potential to be life-changing. Learn more at www.-goalfree.com

**Personality Poker®:** Contrary to conventional wisdom, opposites don't always attract. As a result, organizations hire and retain people who think alike. Although this uniformity is great for efficiency, it can stifle innovation. The key to high-performing innovation teams is ensuring that each individual is "playing to their strong suit" while the organization is "playing with a full deck."

Personality Poker is an interactive game that uses specially crafted cards. They look like regular playing cards, with one exception: each card also has a word representing a particular behavior, such as "creative," "analytical," "organized," and "empathetic." With fifty-two unique cards carrying fifty-two different descriptors, every element in Personality Poker–from the suits and colors to the numbers–has significance. Players trade cards to collect a hand of five that best reflects their self-perception. Additionally, players can "gift" cards to others. Based on the suits, colors, and numbers in your hand, you will discover:

- Your preferred innovation personality
- Your innovation unconscious biases
- The people who you need to complement your hand yet most likely will avoid
- What is missing from your team that is limiting innovation and success
- The culture of your organization and its impact on innovation
- How others perceive you and why any difference from your own perception can be damaging

...and much more.

Learn more at www.personalitypoker.com

---

## SERVICES

There are many ways that we can work together, and this list keeps evolving.

**Keynote Speeches** - For the past twenty-five years, I have delivered speeches in fifty countries. In 2015, I had the honor of being inducted into the Speaker Hall of Fame. My speeches extend beyond mere presentations. We conduct live hot seats, applying the concepts directly to your organization's real-world challenges in real time. Plus, all attendees receive materials that help keep the conversation going long after the event ends. Learn more at www. theinnovationspeaker.com

**The FAST Innovation® Mastery Program** - This is the most powerful and effective way to create a culture of innovation.

Through our proven apprenticeship model, employees not only master the innovation process but also apply it to their daily work, addressing real-world problems. This approach not only enhances employee competency but also yields tangible ROI for your organization. Learn more at www.fastinnovationmastery.com

**FAST Innovation® Academy** - If you are not quite ready for the FAST Innovation Mastery Program, our Academy offers access to our entire content library without extensive guidance. This is ideal for organizations with tighter budgets or those aiming to quickly distribute the content to a broad segment of their organization. You can always upgrade to the Mastery in the future or add on levels of support. This program is under development. If you are interested in learning more, please get in touch with us at inquiries@stephen shapiro.com.

While browsing my website, please explore the various services I offer, including workshops, consulting, advisory services, and more.

# ABOUT THE AUTHOR

As I write these words about my past experiences, I realize two things: 1) This is of more interest to me than you, and 2) Because of that, I don't expect you to continue reading. However, for the few interested in learning more about how I got to where I am, read on.

My career started after I earned a degree in Industrial Engineering from Cornell University. My focus was on improving manufacturing productivity. Although I didn't know it then, this was the perfect field of study for the work I would eventually do.

Right out of college, I joined Arthur Andersen's Management Consulting Division (now Accenture, the global management consulting firm). My first big career opportunity came in 1993 when I helped run our Business Process Reengineering practice. This optimization work was a natural build on my Industrial Engineering work. Instead of improving manufacturing productivity, we focused on improving business productivity.

After a few years of promoting this work, I experienced an existential crisis when I realized that our process improvement work had led to massive downsizing. After a leave of absence during which I evaluated what I wanted to do with my life, I realized I wanted to help companies grow. And since 1996, innovation has been my focus.

At that time, I was fortunate to be given the opportunity to found and lead a process and innovation practice of 20,000 people. I gave speeches and workshops to consultants and clients around the world, promoting our perspectives on innovation. In 2001, I made a shift. I wrote my first book, *24/7 Innovation: A Blueprint for Surviving and Thriving in an Age of Change* (McGraw-Hill). At that time, I left Accenture and branched out on my own.

Since then, I've written six additional books–including the one you hold in your hands.

I have had the luxury of traveling the world, giving speeches in more than fifty countries. And in 2015, I was bestowed one of the highest honors of the speaking profession: I was inducted into the Speaker Hall of Fame.

When not speaking on stage, I practice my not-so-sleight-of-hand magic on my family and friends. Among my greatest celebrity coups, I met my childhood idol, former *Gong Show* host Chuck Barris. And in 2017, I got to be a judge and mentor on the TLC innovation reality television show *Girl Starter*.

I now live in Orlando, Florida, where I enjoy the most amazing life with my wife.

Printed in Great Britain
by Amazon